THE ENGLISH ACHILLES

Engraved portrait of John Talbot

(From *Vrais Portraits des Hommes Illustres,* by G. A. Thevet)

THE
ENGLISH ACHILLES

An Account of the Life and Campaigns of
JOHN TALBOT, 1st EARL OF SHREWSBURY
(1383 — 1453)

By
HUGH TALBOT
With an Introduction by
C. V. WEDGWOOD

1981
CHATTO & WINDUS
LONDON

Published by
Chatto & Windus Ltd
40 William IV Street
London WC2N 4DF
*
Clarke Irwin & Co Ltd
Toronto

British Library Cataloguing in Publication Data
Talbot, Hugh
The English Achilles.
1. Talbot, John *Earl of Shrewsbury*
2. England -- Nobility -- Biography
I. Title
942.04'1' 0924   DA247.S/

ISBN 0 7011 2574 8

Printed in Great Britain by
T. H. Brickell & Son Ltd, Shaftesbury, Dorset

To
THE TALBOT FAMILY

"If an English Commander could ever be so honoured, the deeds performed by John Talbot in the interminable wars between the French and the English must have immortalised him among his countrymen".

G. A. Thevet, 1584

"But where's the great Alcides of the field, Valiant Lord Talbot, Earl of Shrewsbury?"

Shakespeare, *Henry VI, Part I,* Act 4, Scene 7

"How it would have joyed brave Talbot, the terror of the French, to think that, after he had lyne two hundred years in his Tombe, he should triumph again on the stage, and have his bones new embalmed with the teares of ten thousand spectators at least, at severall times, who in the Trajedian that represents his person, imagine that they behold him fresh bleeding".

Thomas Nashe, 1592

CONTENTS

ILLUSTRATIONS

MAPS

INTRODUCTION

The last battle of the Hundred Years War was fought in July 1453 at Castillon, about thirty miles from Bordeaux. The English commander was John Talbot, Earl of Shrewsbury, for many years the most famous of the English captains in France. By this time a veteran of more than seventy, he was killed with his son, making an heroic last stand against overwhelming numbers.

The French had long respected Talbot. France's most chivalrous soldier, Dunois, insisted that full military honours be paid to his body. Even the King, Charles VII — not the most generous of monarchs — prayed "May God have mercy on the good knight". A chapel was built to mark the site of his death. It was destroyed in the French Revolution but Talbot was still remembered, and on the 500th anniversary of the battle, in 1953, a new monument was set up to his memory in the place where he died, on a low grassy mound not far from the swift-flowing Dordogne.

I came on this accidentally some years ago. Returning from a motoring holiday in France, making for Bordeaux and the airport, a signpost caught my eye, pointing down a side road. "Monument Talbot" it said. Monument Talbot? I slowed down at once. This required investigation. It was a long time since I had known much about the Hundred Years War, having spent most of my adult life in the seventeenth century — so much so that even the name of Castillon on the road-map had meant nothing to me. But the name of Talbot I did remember.

The road traversed some wide open fields and came at last close to the tree-lined banks of the splendid river. There I found a grey stone column inscribed in French to "le général John Talbot". A wreath had evidently been laid there very recently, for it was hardly withered. The month was July: it was a few days only after the anniversary of the battle.

I am a great lover of memorials and tombstones of all kinds, and I stood there trying to recall all that I knew of Talbot's life and death. It was shamefully little. Shakespeare's poignant scene in *Henry VI, Part I* was the strongest recollection, for

1

what devotee of Shakespeare can forget the agonising plea of the aged father to his son, to flee from the battle and save his own life, or the young man's resolute refusal to obey?

This incident — as readers of this excellent biography will find out — is true. It is true also that the young man who would not desert his father was killed a few moments before him. But Shakespeare exercised poetic licence in the dying speech of Talbot over his son. Crushed by the fall of his horse, Talbot was beyond speech and may well have been unconscious of his son's death. The terrible turmoil of the battle is vividly — but also *intelligibly* — described in one of the best chapters of this most interesting book. Standing by the monument on that brilliant July day I remembered Shakespeare but I wish I had also known the full story as I know it now.

Talbot's fame long outlasted his death. The French called him the "English Achilles" while the English compared him to Hercules — "the Great Alcides of the field". Though the Elizabethans were rich in heroes of their own, they looked back with pride and admiration to Talbot and his famous deeds in Ireland and France. But even the greatest martial fame diminishes with the passing of the centuries, with newer wars and more recent heroes. By the late eighteenth century Talbot had ceased to be the national figure he had once been. By the time the *Dictionary of National Biography* was compiled, the editors apparently saw nothing strange in assigning the article on Talbot to a distinguished mediaeval scholar who had no great interest in military history. His lengthy account of Talbot, though good on land tenure and administration, is uninspiring and concludes with a disparaging comment on his career in arms. In Bernard Shaw's *Saint Joan* we find him dismissed as "mad bull Talbot", a wholly misleading estimate.

This biography corrects the record. Its author does full justice to Talbot's dash and daring which occasionally led to errors but was far more often successful, as on the Welsh borders and in Ireland. But he also does justice to Talbot's skill and strategy, his careful organisation, and the confidence he inspired in his men.

Though his services to the Crown began under Richard II, and he was in his youth a friend of Prince Hal, when the prince became King he did not take Talbot with him on the

Agincourt campaign. He seems to have distrusted Talbot's connection with Sir John Oldcastle and the heretic Lollards, and probably for that reason sent him away to govern Ireland. Talbot, therefore, whose later fame was all in France, was excluded from the triumph of Henry V.

Talbot's gifts were not, however, exclusively military. He was a good administrator and an intelligent and flexible landowner on his own large estates, during a period of considerable social unrest. There are many points of great interest in Hugh Talbot's full and balanced picture of a neglected but important figure of the late middle ages. I have greatly enjoyed it and profited by it, and most warmly recommend it to all who are seriously interested in history in its human aspects.

C. V. Wedgwood

ACKNOWLEDGEMENTS

I began my researches into the life of my ancestor casually many years ago on learning of some which had been conducted by my cousin, the late General Sir Reginald Talbot. It appeared that, while Military Attaché in Paris, he had been blackballed for membership of a celebrated club on the grounds that he was descended from 'that Talbot who had been responsible for the death of Jeanne d'Arc'. His researches were partly directed towards proving that this was not the case. The papers which he left to me relating to his visit to Castillon in 1892, his correspondence with various French authoritative personalities including Le Général Commandant, Hotel des Invalides, and the various papers handed to him by the Reverend W. E. Egerton, Rector of Whitchurch, and a member of the Shropshire Archaeological and Natural History Society, constituted my initial sources and I have used them freely, particularly the latter. It is a pleasure to acknowledge my indebtedness to the members of that Society past and present.

Over a period of years I was given help by so many people that I can only acknowledge it in a general way; there were the visits to Record Offices and Libraries on my behalf by members of my family and hours of typing from an ever-growing pile of notes. But it was when I read Colonel A. H. Burne's book, *The Agincourt War*, that my casual studies became a more serious study of contemporary accounts of John Talbot. I had to find out whether he was Bernard Shaw's 'mad Bull' or Colonel Burne's hero 'who must be bracketed with Marlborough and Napoleon'.

As my researches deepened my demands widened and I was surprised to find how far the help of the staff of the Wiltshire County Library could take me. Mr James Young of the Marlborough Library seemed to be determined never to be defeated by my requests.

Other sources of help were the Trustees of the Kiplin Trust who gave me an indefinite loan of most of the contemporary Chronicles such as Waurin, Hall and Monstrelet; Mr Mark Baker, Keeper of the Archives of Wellington College, who made Rymer's *Foedora* available to me and advised and supported me in many other ways; and Miss Anne Talbot whose 'Notes on the Talbot Family' were invaluable.

But my main debt of gratitude, which is deep indeed, is due to the late Ian Parsons. My manuscript reached him indirectly through the kindness of friends including Mr Ronald Hamilton, the historian, and there was little occasion for him to take any interest in the amateur writing of a complete stranger. Nevertheless in spite of all his own pre-occupations he took endless pains and spent many generous hours of his time in critical analysis of my work. With infinite patience and tact he coaxed myself and my narrative along the difficult path towards publication, and it is my deep regret that he did not live to see the book in print. Had it not been for his firm and persistent pursuit of that objective the manuscript would certainly not have achieved the honour of being supported by Dame Veronica Wedgwood. Without the enthusiasm brought to bear by those two good people John Talbot, 'the English Achilles', would still be resting in oblivion.

Hugh Talbot
Pewsey, November 1980

CHAPTER I

GOODRICH CASTLE, the home of the Talbot family from the twelfth to the sixteenth century, stands in solid, squat, magnificence on the spur of a hill jutting out into the valley of the River Wye three miles south west of Ross-on-Wye. Built of red-hued sandstone cut from its own surroundings, with its walls flanked by huge round towers, the Castle still gives an impression of impregnable strength. This is increased by the depth of the sheer, rock-faced dry moat which surrounds the landward side. To the west the spur ends in steep cliffs from the top of which the watcher gazes up the river valley into Wales.

The Castle is pre-Norman in origin[1] but was much improved by the conquerors and again, in 1380, by Richard Talbot. He was a devout man who had also founded the Priories of Painswick and, close to Goodrich, Flanesford (now the barn adjoining the farmhouse of that name). Richard Talbot died in 1396 and was succeeded by his eldest son, Gilbert, a year senior to John, who had been born around 1383.

Gilbert had been born at Blackmere Castle near Whitchurch. This alternative home was very different from Goodrich. Although it was surrounded by a deep and generally stagnant moat, it was situated in the fertile fields of Staffordshire and there was no need for bastion strength such as was held by the fortresses on the Welsh and the Scottish borders. It was nevertheless important in being placed on the route from London to Ireland: thirty-five miles or so from Parlgate on the Dee Estuary, whence boats sailed almost daily to Irish ports. It was also on one of the main routes north and south down the west side of the Pennines.

Blackmere Castle was smaller than Goodrich and, placed on gently sloping ground, it was far too close to the Black Mere which gave off, not only dampness, but a noisome stench as the Castle drained into it. The two Castles were, however, both used intermittently in days when a move had to be made every two months or so as an hygienic necessity. In any case the Talbots had a very strong affection for their northern home.

Goodrich Castle
(Crown copyright. Reproduced with permission of the Controller of
Her Majesty's Stationery Office)

They recruited their servants from Whitchurch and the
surrounding villages and, at the end of his long life, when John
had seen little of Staffordshire for many years, he still insisted
that his personal bodyguard should be recruited from
Whitchurch. It was as "Ricardo Talbot de Blackmere" that
his father had been summoned to Parliament in 1383.

John had a younger brother, Richard, who, according to
the custom of the day, was destined for a clerical life in the
Church.

Gilbert and John were both schooled at an early age in the
hard skills of war and, although it is clear that John developed
a deep appreciation of the arts later in his life, it is equally
clear from his rather laboured signature that he was no hand
with a pen.

M. Thevet describes him at the age of eighteen as "medium
in height and extremely adept. None of his contemporaries
(who included the future King Henry V and Prince John of
Bedford) could compare with him in good looks, wrestling,
archery or horsemanship."[2] Of his restless energy and his
impetuosity there is massive evidence up to the end of his very
long life, and even in his last tragic hours at Castillon. His
skeleton, exhumed some four centuries after his death,

confirms that he was 5′ 10″ in height and strongly built: [3] He is described in 1410, at the age of about twenty seven, as being heavy in build, with irregular features, deep-set eyes and an over-prominent nose; he was reputed to have auburn hair and wide-set blue eyes.

His boyhood, spent hunting the stag, the wild boar and the wolf in the Forest of Dean and the Wye Valley, not only developed him physically but gave him a quick mind and a good eye for country. The eye which could discern the best approach by which to take a stag by surprise was later used with devastating effect against the Welsh, the Irish and the French.

In their hunting, the Talbot brothers were joined by local nobles; John Oldcastle from Almeley, some six years older and already engrossed in wider affairs; the three sons of Henry of Monmouth Earl of Derby: Henry or Hal (one day to become King) three years younger than John Talbot; John of Bedford, six years younger, and Thomas eight. Oldcastle, so much older than the others, was of the boastful type. He was always amusing and devoid of all fear. He had gone to Ireland with King Richard in 1394; a land of impenetrable forests and bogs where the inhabitants did not wear breeches but cloaks wrapped round themselves, and where they rode expertly but without saddles. He had also been North to the Scottish Border and over to France. He could recount how King Charles VI of France had suddenly gone mad as he led his army into Brittany and had pursued his own Heralds across the hot plain near Le Mans until, at last, his knights had managed to overpower him.

Occasionally there came too, to Goodrich, important guests: young Henry's grandfather and uncle to the King, the great John of Gaunt, Duke of Lancaster — serious, kindly and always appearing to have, as was the fact, some weighty matter on his mind. His brother, the Duke of Gloucester, was a rather less welcome guest. He was rich and mean and he bullied those who fawned around him. The most important visitor was King Richard himself: a slender, dandified figure, all smiles and charm one moment but in a tearing rage the next. Since the death of his wife, Anne, in 1394 he seemed to prefer to surround himself with sycophants of a rather unpleasant type and, it was said, of even more unpleasant

GENEALOGICAL TABLE OF THE TALBOTS 1350-1470

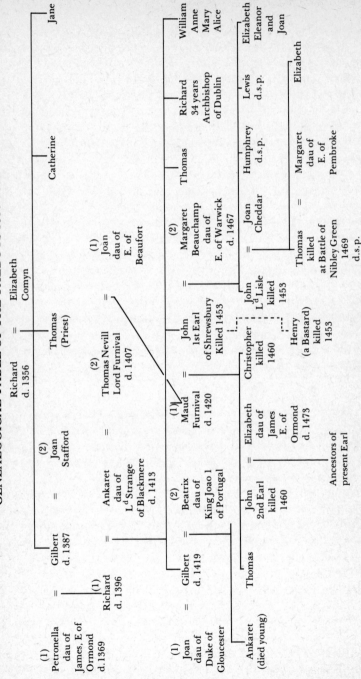

morals. [4]

It was probably with mixed feelings of pleasure at being launched into the world, and dislike of the King and many of those around him, that John learned in 1395 that he was required to attend on the King as a Page.

On arrival at Windsor he found everyone pre-occupied with the arrangements for the King's journey to meet Charles VI, who was now temporarily sane. There, in France, King Richard was to take as his wife the little eight-year-old Princess Isabella. During the latter part of 1394 he had been negotiating for this marriage, so as to cement the truce with France and turn it into a lasting peace. The matter could only be pursued in the short lucid intervals which King Charles had between his bouts of insanity, but by the summer of 1396 all was arranged. King Richard himself was delighted, but his uncles of Lancaster and York were doubtful of the wisdom of an alliance which would admit the right of the House of Valois to claim sovereignty over France. That right was strenuously denied by most English nobles. None was more displeased, or showed it more openly, than the Duke of Gloucester. His dour dislike of his nephew and of the policy he followed became even more pronounced. However, he did agree to accompany Richard to France and in September the whole glittering cavalcade crossed from Sandwich to Calais.

There, for a month, the English in the Pas de Calais and the French around St. Omer staged rival festivities. Feasts, jousting tournaments and sports between the English and French Cvourts were held in all the Monasteries and Houses round about. Young John Talbot even achieved some early renown in defeating all contestants, either French or English, of his own age at both wrestling and archery.

Meanwhile the detailed arrangements for the momentous meeting of the two sovereigns were finalised, and it took place on October 28th, 1396. On that day young Henry of Monmouth, John of Bedford and John Talbot met some of those who in future years they were to know only as adversaries in war. It almost seems in retrospect as if they paraded there across the stage before the curtain rose.

The first meeting between the two Kings was a mere formality. They took spices together and then each cavalcade returned to its own lines. The main meeting took place at 11

o'clock the next morning. King Richard moved again in
stately procession, with his Knights and Esquires in attendance, to dine in state with King Charles. The two Kings were
served by the three Royal Dukes of France—Berry, Burgundy
and Bourbon, a unique proceeding for the youthful John
Talbot to observe at close quarters. At the end of dinner, when
the wine and spices had been placed on the table, came the
climax of the whole occasion. Princess Isabella was led into the
tent. Not only the little Princess but most of the twenty
Ladies-in-Attendance were weeping bitterly. King Charles
took her by the hand and formally "gave" her to King
Richard.

Richard brought the distressing scene to an end and
departed as quickly as possible, taking his tearful little
"Queen" with him in a litter, accompanied by just one French
attendant, Lady De Coucy. Language did not present any
difficulty, for, although most of the English nobility had
talked English among themselves, they were equally conver-
sant in French. Nevertheless England was still regarded by the
French as a wild and uncivilised country.

The next day, Tuesday, Richard and Isabella reached
Calais and there, in the Church of St. Nicholas, they were
married by the Archbishop of Canterbury. On Thursday they
crossed the Channel to Dover, and moved by easy stages to the
Palace of Eltham, which was Richard's favourite home.

It was then that the news reached John Talbot that his
father had died. Gilbert had become the Fifth Baron Talbot,
and John returned home. He was thus not present when
Isabella, still a picture of misery and apprehension, made her
State Entry into London.

On the death of Richard Talbot, Gilbert was a minor and,
until he came of age, was a Ward of Court and his marriage
rights lay with the King. He was already, however, contracted
to wed Joan, daughter of the Duke of Gloucester. The latter's
relationship with his nephew, King Richard, was thus of
considerable interest to the Talbots. It was a relationship
which steadily deteriorated. All attempts by the King, or by
the French during the recent meetings, had failed to win
Gloucester's approval of this reconciliation between England
and France. Richard had even offered Gloucester a peerage
for his son and an annuity for life, but to no avail. Gloucester

had played his official part in the ceremonial but, in doing even that, had managed to make it plain to everyone that he thought nothing of his nephew and heartily disliked any contact at all with the French. Now, on his return to England, he curbed his tongue still less. The whole Court, and especially the King, were relieved when he took himself off to his splendid Castle of Pleshy in Essex.

But the matter could not rest there. Gloucester was not without support in his opposition to the King who, as time went on, surrounded himself with more and more undesirable companions and indulged in more vicious excesses. The day-to-day government went from bad to worse: crime increased and, now that there was no war to occupy them, bands of soldiers roamed the countryside. Many of the nobility, less securely housed than in Castles such as Goodrich, found it safer to move into London or the larger towns.

Gloucester took advantage of this and soon he was claiming that Londoners in particular supported him rather than the King. He became even bolder and, when summoned by the King to Council Meetings, attended or remained absent as the mood suited. Richard's entourage became increasingly apprehensive and many of them made excuses to return to their houses. Amongst these were even such men as Sir Thomas Percy, of that powerful Northern family who, from time to time, had plagued the English government. He had been Steward of the Household for many years, and defections such as his were severe blows to the King's authority.

But the King's other uncles, the Dukes of Lancaster and York, and his brother, the Earl of Huntingdon (who was Governor of Calais), continued to stand by him. With him, too, was Lancaster's son, Henry, Earl of Derby. Much as they disliked Richard and his government, they realised the greater evils which civil war could bring. That was particularly evident at a time when, all over Europe, unrest and strife existed. In Castille, Naples, Flanders and Friesland, rivals were fighting for power and, even in the Church two Popes were trying to claim the Throne of St. Peter. Such divisions must be avoided in England at almost any cost. So, when King Richard asked his uncles how seriously he should oppose Gloucester, they uneasily played down the effects of his plotting and intrigue.

But the King had another source of information. His brother Huntingdon, from his position in Calais, had organised an elaborate network of spies, the passage of wool through the Calais Staple providing a most suitable camouflage for agents. It was through these channels that the King learned of more serious intrigues on Gloucester's part. He decided to strike, although he knew that he could not rely on any of the senior nobility for aid.

On the pretext of hunting he went to his Lodge at Havering-in-the-Bower, some twenty miles from London and the same distance from Pleshy. In the evening, accompanied by only a small party, he rode over to Pleshy, arriving there at 5 o'clock unannounced. Gloucester had just finished his supper and went out with ill grace to greet the King and, most grudgingly, to ask if he had supped. The King drew him aside and told him that he wanted him to come at once to London as he was the only person who could deal with the situation that had arisen there; the City Counsellors had demanded an audience next morning. It was therefore urgent that Gloucester himself should come at once with only his personal servants: the rest of his retinue could follow next morning. [5]

As Richard expected, Gloucester's vanity was flattered and he saw this as yet another opportunity to demonstrate the superiority of his power over that of his nephew. As dusk fell they took the road to London accompanied by only three of Gloucester's Esquires and four of his varlets.

They were trotting their tired horses through the little village of Stratford in the dark when they suddenly found themselves surrounded by horsemen. The King put spurs to his horse and galloped ahead, but Gloucester, taken completely by surprise, was held. To his even greater surprise he saw in the light of torches that his assailants were not brigands but soldiers, led by the Earl Marshal. He imagined that he was to be killed there and then and asked that he might see a Priest before he died; but Norfolk reassured him and told him he was to be taken to the Tower. When they reached London, however, he was put on board a ship anchored out in the river and, by dawn, were far out to sea. They arrived at Calais that evening.

Huntingdon treated his uncle as an honoured guest, but one under constraint. Richard had been too clever to order his

Uncle to be executed until he was sure that his blow against the opposition had succeeded. It had done so perfectly. Arundel and Warwick had been taken into custody at the same time: Arundel had been executed and Warwick, then an old man, had been banished. Within a few days Gloucester was murdered by four men who rushed in on him as he sat at dinner. The King immediately confiscated the whole of his estate. The Duchess of Gloucester and her daughter Joan were in disgrace and became virtually prisoners as Ladies-in-Waiting to Queen Isabella in Leeds Castle, Kent.

The King's action served only to exacerbate opposition to him. Even Lancaster and York felt that they could no longer defend him and they hurried to London. Richard ordered the City gates to be shut against them but, instead, the Londoners turned out to give them an enthusiastic welcome. Richard, expecting an attack to be organised, had returned to Eltham with a force of some 10,000 men and what remained of his Court. This included the Earl Marshal and Henry, Earl of Derby. When the news came of Gloucester's murder a murmur of horror ran through the Court. Henry of Derby was heard to exclaim: "Saint Mary! Fair cousin, what thinketh the King our cousin to do? Will he drive out of England all the noblemen? Within a while there shall be none left."[6] The Earl Marshal passed this on to the King, who decided to take no action then but let matters simmer down before striking again. 1397 came to a close on a note of suppressed unrest and indignation at King Richard's treachery, and the licentiousness of his entourage. John Talbot was then fourteen years old.

On Palm Sunday of 1398 Richard decided to strike another blow at those whom he regarded as dangerous. It was customary on that day for the King to hold a Feast for the Princes of the Royal Blood. Acting, almost certainly, on the King's orders, Norfolk, the Earl Marshal loudly accused Henry of Derby of being a traitor. The latter leapt to his feet and challenged Norfolk to a duel, which was exactly what King Richard had hoped he would do; however, he let it appear that he was much upset and left the banqueting table before the wine and spices were brought.

Excitement surged through the country and it was noticeable that most of the Barons and all the chief citizens of London were whole-heartedly in sympathy with Henry of

Derby. Both antagonists made elaborate preparations for the duel, Henry even going so far as to send to the Duke of Milan for special armour.[7] But there were many who saw the duel as a most unwise affair, and they were led by the Duke of Lancaster. Times were bad enough already: the plague was ravaging the country, making labour so scarce that men could hire their work for money rather than render their enfieffed service. Food was scarce and prices were rising. Lancaster and those closest to the King urged him to unite rather than disrupt the country. For many weeks he made no move, but at last he was persuaded to act. He summoned Derby and Norfolk before him in Council, but separately so that they should not meet. He banished Norfolk, his erstwhile confidant, for life, and Derby for ten years. Norfolk left at once to go and live in Venice. Derby called on the King a fortnight later to say farewell to him, and to his sons who were Esquires at the Court. The King, probably under persuasion from the Council, reduced his banishment to one of six years. As he rode out over London Bridge 40,000 of London's citizens cheered him on his way, and the Lord Mayor himself rode with him as far as Dartford to ensure that there was no treachery before he sailed from there to France.

Early in 1399 the Duke of Lancaster died, and the country mourned him. The ordinary citizen had looked on him as a restraining influence on the King, whose debt to him for faithful service and sound advice was inestimable and well known. So the callousness with which the King took the news of his death shocked many people. They were even more dismayed to learn that Richard had seized the Duchy of Lancaster. Property was sacrosanct even in those violent days, and such a seizure was a crime. More than any other act it sealed King Richard's fate.

The death in battle of the Earl of March, Viceroy of Ireland, in June of 1398 finally precipitated matters. The native Irish had gradually been pressing the English Colonists back within narrower limits around Dublin. Richard's attempt to come to terms with them in 1394 had failed miserably and, if the Colony was now to be saved at all, it seemed to the King that he must take an army over himself. Perhaps he also felt that it would deflect attention from the state of affairs in England.

In April 1399 he sent out orders for the levies to muster at Bristol in June. The more Northern nobles, including the Percys, refused point blank. Those nearer the point of muster had no alternative but to obey, and Gilbert and John Talbot both did so with their levy of 40 men-at-arms and 80 archers. So far as is known, that was the first of John's many indentures for service. It is merely recorded[8] that John Talbot "acquitted himself right manfully", but his first major campaign taught him many lessons, mainly of a negative nature. The army which assembled at Bristol numbered some 2,000 men-at-arms and 10,000 archers, together with a vast throng of horses, cows, wagon-loads of salted meats, casks of fresh water, crates of bowstrings and arrows and other stores.[9] But pilfering was widespread and discipline very bad. This did not improve as the long, cumbersome column wound its way through the hostile Welsh countryside to Milford Haven. There followed a wait of ten days for a favourable wind. The King had joined them and had caused considerable amusement by bringing with him the full Royal Regalia and Jewelry. It was even rumoured that he had on his person the Ampulla of consecrated oil used at his Coronation.[10] (This Ampulla is said to be the oldest item in the Coronation Regalia still in use today.) With him, too, were two of his evil cronies: the Bishop of Carlisle and Father Maudelain. The latter was so like King Richard that he could, and often did, impersonate him — a joke which the King much enjoyed.

The transports anchored eventually in Waterford Harbour on June 1st, but a further week elapsed before the army had disembarked and was ready to move. Richard then marched to Kilkenny, the home of his friend the Earl of Ormond. There he waited a further fortnight for the Duke of Albemarle, who had been retained to serve him with a further 140 men-at-arms and 200 mounted archers. The Duke never arrived, and, on June 23rd, the King decided that he could wait no longer; he marched west into Leinster. It was wild country dominated by a fierce and astute Irish Chieftain called Art Oge MacMurragh. During Richard's campaign in 1396, Art, styled King of Leinster, had allowed himself, together with his fellow Kings of Meath, Thomond and Connaught, to be taken to Dublin. There Richard had tried to

Anglicise them. He had them placed in the care of Sir John
Froissart, the Chronicler. The latter had been captured by the
Irish and had spent seven years among them; he had married
an Irish wife and spoke the language. Thus he was well
qualified for the task the King gave him. But he could make
no impression upon them: he records that he could not induce
them to wear breeches instead of mantles, or to put harness on
their horses. They even insisted on eating their meals with
their servants; Richard had somewhat reluctantly knighted
them. Art, a sardonic man of commanding presence, had
returned, unchanged, to his native Leinster and had continued to war against the English settlers. Now, after a lapse of
three years, Richard was determined to bring him to
submission.

It was not perhaps surprising that as the cumbersome
English forces moved forward, they met no opposition and all
the huts they came across were empty. They burned the huts
and struggled on, knowing that an unseen enemy was
watching them. Parties sent off to forage never returned, and
whole herds of cows disappeared overnight. As they penetrated deeper into hostile country their difficulties increased
and soon provisions began to run low. To add to their troubles
the weather was appalling: there were incessant gales and
rain. It was not lost upon young John Talbot that a high
degree of mobility and excellent discipline were both essential
in combating local bands of armed men. Eventually Richard
recognised the futility of his campaign and headed his ragged
and demoralised army north towards Dublin. Derisory shouts
followed them from the hillsides. [11]

It was a relief to reach civilisation again and, in the relative
plenty of Dublin, to forget the hardships they had endured.
Moreover the King found the Duke of Albemarle waiting for
him there. Richard was too weary and too pleased to see him
to be angry, though he repeatedly asked the Duke the reason
for his failure to arrive at Kilkenny. The gales and storms
which had made life so difficult in the forests of Kilkenny had
also prevented any ships crossing the Irish Sea for six
weeks. [12] The first one arrived on August 3rd and it brought
startling news. Henry of Derby had landed at Ravenspur in
Yorkshire, and was trying to raise the country against the
King.

The news of Derby's landing electrified the army. Several nobles and their musters disappeared overnight, and were later found to have crossed the sea by a northern route to join the insurrection.

One of Richard's first actions was to send young Henry of Monmouth, in the care of Humphrey of Gloucester, to Trim Castle in County Meath and some thirty miles from Dublin. [13] At the same time he called a meeting of his Council, at which he announced that he intended to sail from Howth (a harbour close to Dublin) on the following Monday, August 5th. The Council, however, consisted of the Earl of Salisbury, the Duke of Albemarle, the Duke of Exeter, the Bishops of Lincoln and Carlisle and the Abbot of Westminster. Of these at least three were in the plot to bring Henry of Derby back to England, though it was chiefly Albemarle who argued with the King privately: [14] "Sire do not vex yourself, for never did I hear a matter so much belied. Be not in such haste now to set out . . ." It was indeed relatively easy to persuade Richard that it would be best if he delayed his own crossing, and sent Salisbury ahead to raise troops and to attack Derby. Having been in recent touch with Derby, Albemarle knew that this would give Derby sufficient time to consolidate his position in England.

So, while Salisbury sailed from Howth, Richard marched what was left of his army to Wexford, where the transports lay. The embarkation was so badly organised that the King did not reach Milford Haven until a fortnight later. Even then he had few troops with him; he found no army awaiting him, no word from Salisbury, and only the alarming information that Derby was near Oxford with a powerful force.

In fact, soon after Salisbury's arrival in England, a faked message had been delivered to him saying that King Richard had been killed. Salisbury had thereupon gone into hiding to await the outcome of events. Another supporter of the King who also disappeared was Father Maudelain, but he had the forethought to take with him the contents of the Irish Treasury. [15]

There is no evidence as to how Gilbert and John Talbot met this crisis, but it is hard to believe that their sympathies were not wholly with Derby and his sons. The probability is that they returned to Goodrich and were there during the dramatic events of the next few weeks. News no doubt filtered through to them of the King's capture in Conway Castle, of his ignominious journey to London under the escort of Henry of Derby, or Henry Duke of Lancaster as he now claimed to be called; and later of King Richard's abdication in favour of Henry in the great Hall of Westminster.

On Wednesday, September 30th, 1399, Parliament passed a Resolution making Henry, Duke of Lancaster, King, and on October 13th he was crowned. At the Coronation Ceremony, Lord Furnival (whose title John Talbot was later to inherit), "by reason of his Manor of Ferneham with the hamlet of Cere",[16] gave to the King a glove for his right hand, a privilege which is still enjoined on present holders of the title at the coronation of the Sovereign.

CHAPTER II

FOR SEVERAL DAYS after the Coronation there was feasting and dancing in the streets of London, and in towns and villages up and down the country. But for the new King there was much work to be done and many problems to be resolved.

The country would expect swift justice to be meted out to those who had supported King Richard's last years of misrule. The question was what should be done with them and, even more importantly, what should be done with Richard himself. Henry wisely decided that leniency should be exercised. The late King was taken in disguise from the Tower to Pontefract Castle. The Earl of Salisbury was imprisoned but not executed. The hot-blooded Percy family were appeased by the elevation of their head as Earl of Northumberland, and his appointment as Earl Marshal in place of the disgraced Norfolk.

But perhaps the most intricate problem was what should be done with Queen Isabella. She was still in Leeds Castle in Kent, where Richard had left her when he set off on his ill-fated adventure in Ireland. France could only be offended at Richard's eclipse but if, in addition, his wife was sent back to France, her very substantial dowry would also have to be returned. This the Exchequer could not afford.

The obvious course was for her to marry Prince Henry, who was deeply in love with her. But this was out of the question both because her husband was still alive and, equally pertinently, because Isabella herself would not even see Prince Henry, far less entertain the idea of marriage to him. The Council decided that she should be kept in England for the present, as a pawn to hold the French in check. They sent Lady de Coucy back to France, telling her to take care that on leaving the Queen she should show no signs of anger at being dismissed, and to pretend that she had been sent for from France. An entirely new household now surrounded the miserable little girl and, a stipulation which added to her misery, they were forbidden even to mention the name of the erstwhile King. It was thus Lady de Coucy who was the first to carry back to France authentic news of Richard's abdication. King Charles immediately went into such a rage that it brought on another fit of madness. The Duke of Burgundy merely remarked that he had always thought that Isabella's marriage was a mistake but that, possibly, with Richard of Bordeaux now in custody, the people of Bordeaux might throw off their years of English allegiance. His hopes were not to be fulfilled.

The hopes of the people of England that the advent of Henry IV would bring peace and plenty were likewise doomed to disappointment. Huntingdon, always an intriguer, could not resist the temptation of conspiracy. To add fuel to his zeal the shadowy Father Maudelain re-appeared, still carrying with him much of the contents of the Irish Treasury wnich he had emptied, so he said, by the royal command. [1] That first Christmas of the new King's reign Huntingdon, Maudelain and others staged an elaborate insurrection. The plot's scenario included the murder of the King and his sons, who were at Windsor, followed by a triumphal march headed by Father Maudelain impersonating Richard, the liberated and rightful King. The venture nearly succeeded, in spite of betrayal by the Earl of Rutland. The Royal family, suffering from some form of stomach trouble, had to gallop through a stormy winter night from Windsor Castle to the safety of London. The insurgents were eventually liquidated by the good people of Cirencester who then, as evidence of their good deed, sent "two panniers full of rebel flesh" to the King in London.

The insurrection and the continuous rumours as to Richard's movements, although he was by now incarcerated in Pontefract, intensified the pressure on the King to do away with his rival. But he had promised his cousin that he would not harm him and, being a man of deep religious devotion and integrity, it is unlikely that he ever seriously considered doing so. Nevertheless in February 1400 Richard died, and the cause of his death remains unknown. Froissart, the contemporary Chronicler, tried by every means to discover it, but failed. Probably only the men of the garrison at Pontefract Castle ever knew the truth — and they held their peace.

The death of Richard did little to ease the problems which confronted King Henry. Threatening moves by the French forced him to reinforce the garrisons of Calais, Guisnes, and neighbouring castles. Under pressure from France the Scots were preparing to attack him from the north, aided, as some said, by the Percys. There were stirrings too in North Wales, where rebellion was never far below the surface. Finances were highly strained. Henry was determined not to follow his cousin's example of extortionate taxes levied without Parliamentary authority, but Parliament was equally determined to reduce taxation to the minimum. The result was that, throughout his reign, Henry lived personally in the most stringent poverty and expected his sons to do so too.

It was now the Spring of 1400. John Talbot was about 17 years old, Prince Henry 14, and Prince John of Bedford 12. But manhood's responsibilities were acquired early in days when a man was lucky if he attained the age of 50. Boys were given their first swords at the age of ten and were expected to use them to good effect. Marriages were contracted equally early.

Gilbert Talbot had married Gloucester's daughter, Joan, but she had died in childbirth; John Talbot was contracted to marry Maud, the only child of Lord Furnival. He, Furnival, had been recently bereaved and he now married John Talbot's mother, Ankaret.

It was the threatened insurrection in Wales which presented the King with the most serious challenge to his authority, and which imminently affected the Talbots at Goodrich. Wales was then a wild land, but it was occupied by strong feudal landlords who ruled their territories with considerable enlightenment. They were almost all antagonistic to the English, and constant raids and counter-raids took place across the ill-defined Border. It was the duty of Captains of Castles to maintain order as far afield as possible.

Prominent among the large estate owners were the Tudors: Gwilym ap Tudor and his brother Rhys ap Tudor: also their cousin Owain Glyn Dwi, or Owen Glendower as the English called him. He was a tall, bearded, fine-looking man of commanding presence who had, in early days, been apprenticed in the Inns of Court. In 1385 he had fought in King Richard's Scottish campaign. Now, at the age of fifty, he was rich and widely respected.

In August 1400 a bitter quarrel broke out between

Glendower and Lord Grey of Ruthyn, [2] a kinsman of the Talbots and, until recently, Gilbert Talbot's guardian. Grey, although he was English, owned considerable estates in North Wales, bordering on those of Glendower, and minor quarrels were nothing new. This one, however, was different. Glendower alleged that Grey maliciously delayed the service on Glendower of a summons to serve on an expedition which King Henry was planning against Scotland, with the result that Glendower was indicted in his absence as a traitor.

Grey was something of a bully and the story could well have been true. But, whatever the reason, it so embittered Glendower that, from then onwards, he became an implacable enemy of the English. On September 16th he suddenly attacked Ruthyn Castle and burned it to the ground. He went on to ravage the English settlements at Denbigh, Rhuddlan, Flint, Hawarden and Holt. In the full flush of this success he then proclaimed himself Prince of Wales.

The King was at Northampton on his way south from the Scottish Border. He called out the levies of Warwickshire, Shropshire and Staffordshire, which latter included the Blackmere contingent under the Bailiff. After an indecisive skirmish near Welshpool, Glendower retreated into Wales. On September 26th the King joined the army and formally declared Glendower an outlaw, his estates being forfeit. He made a half-hearted sally into Wales, but turned back after a fortnight. It was now October, which was then considered too late for campaigning, a fact of which Glendower was well aware. He himself continued to lord it over North Wales and his lightning-like raids into English territory that winter became legendary. Border castles such as Goodrich had to be maintained at full strength and on a war footing.

Meanwhile trouble of a different nature was brewing in England. Many people had been appalled by the conduct of the Church Hierarchy during Richard's last years as King. Too many of them, Priests and Prelates alike, had been prepared, in their own interests, to condone and even to take part in the vicious excesses of that regime. The Bishop of Carlisle, who had been renowned for his wenching and drunken orgies with Richard, had been quite content to be present at his abdication and to be one of the first to acclaim Henry as King. The wealthy ostentation of the Churchmen sickened people at a time when the lot of the average villager was barely above subsistence level. The fact that this wealth had been acquired, and was being added to, by dubious means, such as the sale of pardons, only made matters worse. Men talked secretly of a revival of the teaching twenty years earlier of Wycliffe and his Lollard followers.

In January 1401, when both Parliament and Church Convocation met, the subject of Lollardy came to the fore. Being a Lollard did not involve membership of a secret society or sect: it was more a way of thought; a realisation that much of Church practice and doctrine had become artificial and even false, and it permeated all stratas of society. It now posed a very real threat to the authority of the established Church, which was determined to crush it. Yet to many of the laity who helped to rule the country it seemed a reasonable philosophy, particularly if the King, possessed of the Church's wealth, could use it instead of having to ask Parliament to levy ever-increasing taxes.

It was said that one out of every two men in London were Lollards, and that the proportions were only slightly less in other big cities up and down the country. The rural areas, being naturally more conservative, were more orthodox, but Herefordshire and Norfolk were both notorious for their advanced free-thinking. The name of John Oldcastle, a near neighbour of the Talbots, frequently cropped up in this connection.

In February of 1401 a case of four confessed Lollards came before Convocation. A Priest called William Sawtry was, after torture, the only one who refused to recant. He stoutly maintained his firm belief that, in the Mass, after Consecration of the Eucharist, the bread did not cease to be bread but "only became holy, true and the Bread of Life". Convocation formally stripped him of his office and could probably have let the matter rest there. But, under pressure from Archbishop Arundel, Parliament went to the length of condemning Sawtry to be publicly burned as a heretic. That hideous and demoralising spectacle was no unusual punishment on the Continent, for political as well as for ecclesiastical offences; but it had never before been practised in England. The wretched man was taken to Smithfield and chained to a stake fastened upright in a barrel heaped with faggots. With great bravery he became even more defiant, thundering out denunciations of the King, the Archbishop and the Pope until, as the flames rose around him, his voice turned to screams before he was finally overcome.

A fortnight later the grim Parliamentary Statute "De Heretico Comburendo" was promulgated. It delegated to Sheriffs of Counties or Mayors of Cities the power to inflict this inhuman punishment. Waves of horror and indignation swept through the country, and one of the loudest voices raised in protest was inevitably that of John Oldcastle. In the light of subsequent events it seems probable that John Talbot's voice, too, was not silent. The statute would certainly not have accorded with his humane nature.

During 1401 the Welsh rebellion continued unabated. In answer to Glendower's call, all Welsh students at Oxford and Cambridge started to make their way back to Wales. Welsh labourers on English farms, which were already short of hands as a result of the plague, were flouting the law by leaving their place of work overnight and furtively returning to their own country. In Wales itself fields lay neglected as the men-folk attended secret training sessions in isolated spots. Welsh stock, too, was being sold in border towns such as Shrewsbury and Hereford, and the vendors were buying bows, arrows, harness and even horses with the proceeds. The rebellion, started locally by Owen Glendower, was becoming a national revolt against English rule.

Nor was the rebellious spirit confined to Wales. In the short space of two years the joyous optimism with which the country had received King Henry had disappeared, and discontent had returned. The state of the country was aptly and fearlessly expressed by Doctor Repyngdon, the Chancellor of Oxford University and a close friend of the King, with whom he had just been staying. In a letter which he addressed to Henry in March, [3] "Law and Justice are in exile," he wrote, "and tyrannous caprice has taken their place: thefts, murders, adulteries abound: the poor are oppressed and all is quarrel and contention. The King's promise to protect his subjects and to defend them against their enemies has been forgotten and those who, two years since, shouted welcome to him as to a Christ triumphant, now stand wringing their hands. The people, like wild beasts without rule or reason, take justice into their own hands; against nature, they seize the reins of Government and range savagely against all classes alike."

"Unless the King will deign to awake to punish their excesses," the letter concluded, "I greatly fear lest the soldiery must interfere and 20,000 be killed before the sword can be put up again".

Near to Goodrich a highwayman called Thomas Blyton kept outlying parts of Herefordshire in a state of terror for many weeks, and such happenings could be endlessly multiplied. Parliament issued Decrees to meet the general lawlessness, setting up County Commissions with very wide powers of arrest and dismissal: even Sheriffs could be relieved of their appointment if found to be inefficient. Further Decrees were aimed at the Welsh threat. No one born in Wales was allowed to purchase or to hold land or property in Chester, Shrewsbury, Bridgnorth, Ludlow, Leominster, Hereford, Gloucester or Worcester, or their suburbs, or to become a citizen or burgess of those towns. Any already so enrolled were to be bound to give security for good behaviour, and anyone having a Welsh tenant was to be held responsible for his good behaviour. Any Welshman convicted of plundering in any English County or of attempting to escape to Wales was to be dealt with summarily by the Lords of the Marches. In practice, this meant summary execution, and for the next three years no Englishman could be convicted in Wales on information laid by a Welshman.

A second lengthy Ordinance, issued on March 22nd, 1401, dealt with Welshmen in Wales. It placed them under what would today be called "Martial Law" summarily exercised by Captains of Castles. Bards and Minstrels were severely restricted. This was a measure copied later by John Talbot in Ireland, where Bards were an equally important factor in promoting insurrection as they travelled the country carrying information and preaching resistance to the English.

These Ordinances were designed to give added strength to the mere handful of English, of which Gilbert and John Talbot were part, who had to control the country from their isolated Castles. It was a control which was administered along the length of the Welsh Border on behalf of King Henry by Prince Henry, with a Council and Headquarters at Chester. The Prince's Lieutenant was Henry Percy, eldest son of the

Earl of Northumberland, and nicknamed 'Hotspur': a man of thirty-five, he had long since made his name as an expert raider harrying the Scots, and the King no doubt hoped that Prince Henry would learn much from the older man. But, in the event, his uncertain temperament and indeed his doubtful loyalty made him a difficult henchman for the youthful Prince to manage. In spite of all these measures, Glendower's revolt continued to gain momentum. The fact was that Henry had neither the time nor the resources to mount a serious counter-attack against him.

In November 1401 he even sent letters to "the Lords of Ireland" (which included Art MacMurragh) urging them to send him aid against "our and your deadly foes, the Saxons". [4] The messengers were intercepted and executed but the success of Glendower's tactics did not pass unobserved by the Irish.

In the Spring of 1402 Glendower's success became even more marked. Once again he attacked Ruthyn Castle and, by an immense stroke of luck, actually captured his old enemy, Lord Grey.

The Rules of War of that time, if such they could be termed, were a curious combination of utter brutality, hard commercialism, and extreme chivalry. So far as the war in France was concerned it was, desirably, a profitable business venture in which the King was entitled to a quarter of all prizes at sea and to one third of all "gains of war". These included booty and ransoms: at the top end of the scale prisoners of Royal blood were reserved for the King. [5] Thus, while an ordinary soldier, if taken prisoner, was killed out of hand, a knight or a noble carried an intrinsic ransom value which depended on his rank and his influential standing. He was therefore kept prisoner under reasonably congenial conditions while the matter of ransom was arranged, sometimes by the prisoner himself, sometimes by his relatives. Thus it came about that Lord Grey, a man of influence, was ransomed by order of the King on 13th October. [6]

In June an even greater prize fell into Glendower's hands. Lord Mortimer, a cousin of the King, marched into Wales with a small army which, rashly, included Welsh mercenary archers. They were at that time probably the finest soldiers in Europe and it was their skill with the bow which contributed so much to the English victories in France. But on this occasion they turned on their English companions, whereupon Glendower appeared from the surrounding woods, and Mortimer was captured. The two men had known each other in London, and Mortimer made no attempt to have himself ransomed.

The King ordered Prince Henry to attack, and the latter mustered the levies of Shrewsbury, Chester and Hereford. The last named probably included the men of Goodrich. Prince Henry moved fast, even though the weather that September was appalling and the army suffered considerable hardship. On one occasion they took Glendower by surprise, but he just managed to make his escape, and he and his men disappeared into the mountains. In November he married Lord Mortimer's eldest daughter.

That winter of 1402 King Henry tried to enforce a blockade along the entire Welsh Border. This must have greatly exercised the Captains and garrisons of the Border Castles, particularly as the blockade was deeply resented by folk on both sides of the Border.

During these years John Talbot acquired much of the skill which he was to demonstrate in years to come, in a rather specialised form of warfare: the skill of rapid movement, often at night, in an attempt to catch the elusive enemy unawares. In addition, those weeks and months of sporadic campaigning undoubtedly built up a close personal relationship between those taking part. They were comparatively few in number and they constantly exchanged information as well as personal views. Names that occur and re-occur are John Greindor, Lord Grey, Lord Somerset, John Fairfield, John Skidmore, William Newport, John Oldcastle and, of course, Prince Henry. All these would know quite intimately what each other's views, temperament and ability added up to, and this probably applied particularly to those of the younger generation.

The relationship was further cemented when, in March 1403, the King formally appointed Prince Henry Governor of Wales with power of command over the Welsh Marches. [7] He also gave him Cheylesmore Castle near Coventry as part of the Duchy of Cornwall. There the Prince, now seventeen years old, held Court.

His father's poverty, numerous worries and physical tired-
ness reacted on the young Prince, making him wild, gay and
not a little reckless. He and John Talbot still had much in
common; they were both good athletes, Prince Henry being
faster but Talbot having greater staying power. They were
both impulsive by nature, though whereas Prince Henry's
temper occasionally got the better of him, Talbot's did not.
Neither of them knew what fear was and both of them had an
inborn sense of justice and fair play. To Cheylesmore many
young men resorted between their military duties, and there
enjoyed themselves. [8] There was no shortage of girls, of wine
and of good company. But most of the wildness was of the
dare-devil variety rather than the sensual: midnight races on
horseback; absurd competitions such as entering some Castle
unobserved to win a wager; even stealing someone's horse and
returning it next day with an appropriate message. There were
several occasions when, in disguise, they carried out highway
robberies, followed by liberal rewards to those servants,
particularly Royal ones, who put up a good fight.

But on at least one occasion things went badly wrong. This
was the night on which they decided to test the Coventry
defences, which were a great deal more effective than they
expected. All of them, including Prince Henry, were taken
into custody and charged with raising a riot. The Mayor
reported this incident to the King. On another occasion Prince
Henry even saw the inside of a London gaol on a charge of
"Contempt of Court".

It was all harmless enough but, as more and more reports
reached the King he became convinced that Prince Henry had
become completely irresponsible. This conviction deepened as
the King's health deteriorated, and an unbridgeable gulf
opened between father and son. It was a tragic gulf, for those
who knew the Prince well, knew, too, how much he loved and
admired his father.

In July 1403 Henry Hotspur defected and collected an army
with which he hoped to unite Welsh and Scottish forces. The
battle of Shrewsbury followed, in which Hotspur was killed.
John Talbot's future father-in-law, Lord Furnival, was given
the task of disposing of Hotspur's body. He gave it temporary
burial at Whitchurch where, fifty years later, John Talbot's
heart was to be interred and where his bones now rest. Prince

Henry "was sore wounded in the face with an arrow"[9] which left a scar of which he was always ridiculously proud, for it was his first wound in battle.

After the battle of Shrewsbury the King hurried north to help the Earl of Westmorland put an end to the Percy revolt. The Earl of Northumberland capitulated and, although King Henry deprived him of his somewhat short-lived office of Constable and confiscated much of his lands, he survived. Meanwhile, however, Glendower had appeared in the upper valley of the River Towy and, with general support, had made his victorious way past Llandilo and Dryslwyn to Carmarthen, a key fortress which surrendered to him on July 6th. To add to the King's difficulties Glendower had succeeded in obtaining aid from King Charles. A small French fleet under Jean d'Espagne sailed up the Welsh coast and made raids on various Castles. In November Carnarvon was assaulted, then Beaumaris and, early in 1404, first Harlech and then Aberystwyth fell. By May of that year Glendower was in such a strong position that he could go so far as to convene a Welsh Parliament to meet at Dolgelly. He and the still fractious Earl of Northumberland and Lord Mortimer then signed a tripartite agreement under which they parcelled out England and Wales between them, defining the territorial boundaries with immense precision.

On December 18th, 1404, when John Talbot was twenty-one, he was appointed Captain of Montgomery Castle. It carried a garrison of 45 men-at-arms and 140 archers[10] and, standing as it did on the threshold of Glendower's territory, it was of considerable importance.

CHAPTER III

AS 1405 OPENED the King was faced with a further attack from the north, where the Earl of Northumberland had, yet again, acquired considerable support, particularly in north Yorkshire, and ever stronger resistance in Wales. In April, Scrope, the Archbishop of York, finally came out in the open in support of Northumberland and what were termed the Cleveland Rebels. Forced, no doubt, by the need to meet attack on two fronts the King, with Prince Henry, moved north. He was accompanied by, amongst others, Lord Furnival, John Talbot's step-father, who was now Lord Treasurer, and who possessed very considerable estates in north Nottinghamshire, Derbyshire and Yorkshire, an area known as Hallamshire. Furnival, like many others, had lent the King large sums of money to finance the operation.

In shocking weather the rebels were defeated at Topcliffe near Thirsk, and Archbishop Scrope was taken prisoner. Under conditions which remain as mysterious as those of the death of Richard II, Scrope was murdered. It was an incident which was to haunt King Henry, a deeply religious man, until his dying day. It may or may not have been due to this that, from then onwards, his health steadily deteriorated. At the time it was said that he had contracted leprosy as he rode across Hessay Moor in the wild wet weather. He arrived back in Hereford on September 4th, looking a broken man, constantly taking drastic medicinal treatment and attended by two doctors, David di Nigarelli and Pietro di Alcobasse. [1]

Meanwhile Glendower had suffered his first defeat and it had been at the hands of Gilbert and John Talbot. A muster of 500 men-at-arms and 2,650 archers had been assembled at Hereford under Prince Henry in preparation for an attack on Rhys Gethin. On the morning of March 11th, a messenger reached Goodrich from Sir John Skidmore, Captain of Grosmont Castle in the upper valley of the River Monnow, to say that a rebel force was about to attack him. It had moved in from Glamorgan and was thought to number some 8,000 men. Grosmont, Hereford and Goodrich together form an almost equal-sided triangle. The Talbots realised that

32

Skidmore could not hold out for long against such a strong force but, typically, with their own puny force of 29 men-at-arms and 150 mounted archers, they decided to go to Skidmore's aid. They were joined en route by both Sir William Newport and Sir John Greindor, with some more men, bringing the total force to about 500 men. Gilbert and John divided the force between them and separated as they reached the top of Serrathin. Gilbert followed the river while John made a detour to the south. Their timing was so accurate that the Welshmen had no idea that they were in danger until the converging attack hit them. The record says that "not a single Welshman was taken alive" and that "the Welsh of the upper valley of the Usk sent in their submission". Prince Henry wrote to his father that both Gilbert and John Talbot had "greatly distinguished themselves in battle against the Welsh".

On March 12th, 1405, John Talbot married Maud Furnival in the great Priory Church at Worksop. Of the various Manors owned by Lord Furnival, which included the small village of Sheffield, Worksop appears to have been the family's favourite home, and prayers have been said in the Priory Church there for Maud and her family until very recently. It was said that she spent many hours in the upper floor of the Gatehouse to the Priory in learned discussion with the Monks, and in watching the spectacle of the Market just below. It would seem that her background of cultural learning would not be likely to accord with that of John Talbot, the hardened soldier.

That same year found Gilbert Talbot complaining, like so many other nobles, that he was heavily in debt and that, in spite of appeals to the King, he could not obtain payment from the Exchequer. He asked whether John could exercise influence on his step-father—cum—father-in-law. The Talbots were not alone in needing cash. That summer the garrison at Calais mutinied; they seized the Stapler's Wool and forced the merchants to buy it from them "as a loan to the King". The plague raged too, and in London alone 30,000 people died.

In March 1407 Lord Furnival died and John Talbot succeeded to the title,[2] to the estates and to the debts owed to Furnival by the Crown. As the years passed these latter steadily increased so that, in his Will, Talbot had to instruct his executor to "sue the King and Lords of his Council for such

debts as are due to me by our said Sovereign Lord, considering
the great cost and injury to my person that I have had in his
service, that my wife and my executors may have my said debts
in performing my Will *without which it cannot be done*"
(author's italics).

During 1407 the King mounted a major offensive in Wales,
Prince Henry being in command. Aberystwyth was besieged,
the King even going so far as to add to the massive siege
artillery his own 4½ ton gun which had to be dragged all the
way from Nottingham. The Castle capitulated in September.

The winter which followed was the hardest for a hundred
years all over Europe. The Garonne froze over at Bordeaux
and the Rhine and the Danube were both icebound for many
weeks. In England the country was covered with snow from
December to March and birds, such as fieldfares, quails, and
plovers, which formed the staple article of food at the
poulterers, died off in thousands. [3]

It was in the month of January of that terrible winter that
the Earl of Northumberland chose to raise his standard yet
again at Thirsk in Yorkshire, in his last fatal venture. He
called on all those who loved liberty to take up arms with him.
He was joined by men, not only from York and Ripon, but
from all the villages nearby: from Helmsley, Osmotherley,
Topcliffe, Silton, Sand Hutton, Sessay, Easingwold and even
by monks from the Abbeys of Rievaulx and Fountains.
However, Sir Thomas Rokeby, Sheriff of Yorkshire, collected
a small force and, on February 19th, 1408 fell upon
Northumberland's small band of rebels at Bramham Park.
The snow was deep and the skirmish sharp and decisive. The
rebels were routed and Northumberland himself was killed.
He was buried in York Minister beside the remains of the
equally rebellious Hotspur.

It was in that hard winter, too, that Gilbert and John were
renewing the siege of Aberystwyth, which finally fell again in
the Spring. In the meantime, however, the two brothers had
been detached from the main force and ordered to lay siege to
Harlech Castle. By December, 1408 they had 300 men-at-
arms, 600 archers and a host of "stone-cutters, carpenters,
blacksmiths, gunners and other labourers", all of them indentured to serve for at least three months. Their wages for this
period totalled £5,249.12s.4d. [4] a substantial amount in

those days.

Harlech was a formidable fortress, being quite impregnable from the seaward side, which made a total blockade difficult. By the Autumn no impression had been made on the defences, and the garrison was not being reduced by famine. The Talbots determined that they would not allow Harlech to defeat them; they argued that, although the sea might provide a life-line in the summer, few supply ships would venture in on that coast during the Winter months, and its blockade would therefore be complete. The men and even the King himself disapproved of such a revolutionary idea as continuing to campaign, in wild country, once the weather had broken. The King even hinted that he might not be able to finance the siege. But Gilbert and John were young and determined and they had their way. Harlech Castle surrendered to them in February 1409. The haggard, starving garrison emerged, led by Mortimer's wife and her four children, Mortimer himself having died in January. Their captors dispatched them to London, but they too died soon after entering the Tower.

That defeat was the beginning of the end for Glendower. His authority waned and he remained a legendary will o' the wisp figure, only capable of provoking minor resistance. Henceforth the work of Captains of Castles such as the Talbots, Greindor and Oldcastle, was to press home English dominance with flying columns. For this purpose Gilbert had 80 men-at-arms and 160 mounted archers at Goodrich and John, at Montgomery, 60 men-at-arms and 140 mounted archers; with these highly trained and mobile forces they could harry any insurgents to a point when they were a negligible threat. One such incident is recorded in which John Talbot carried out a sweep through Carnarvon and, on his way home, sought supplies in Shrewsbury. The town's pro-Welsh Constable shut the gates against him and John had to overcome considerable resistance before he could enter the town and obtain what he required.

The work of these mobile columns, covering as they did the length and breadth of Wales, was co-ordinated and controlled by Prince Henry. The relationship between him and the Border Captains was a very close one. Many of them had known each other from childhood and had now been campaigning together for at least six years. But behind all

relationships in those critical days there lay a dark area of
doubt, if not of actual mistrust. No-one knew for certain who
had or had not Lollard leanings, or, if they had, how deeply
involved they were. The topic was never far below the surface
and John Talbot met it acutely when, on 4th December, 1409,
he was summoned to Parliament for the first time in his new
title of Lord Furnival. [5] John Oldcastle's name appears also
in that Parliament roll under his title of Lord Cobham.

While there was no doubt about Oldcastle's Lollard involve-
ment, the position of young Prince Henry was not at all clear:
some even said he was sympathetic to the Lollards' views and
quoted an incident at Evesham to support this. There a tailor
called John Badby had been accused of heresy, refused to
recant and was condemned to be burned. After the fire had
been lit Prince Henry had had him lifted out of it to be given a
chance to recant. The man had refused and was put back
again, but Prince Henry was thought to have shown him most
significant sympathy.

In 1410 Lord Walsingham, a close friend of Oldcastle,
introduced a Bill in Parliament "to confiscate the wealth of
the Clergy". It was thrown out, but the Ecclesiastical authorities were left in no doubt that their power was under serious
threat. Among many knights who rose to support the Bill was
John Talbot's kinsman, Thomas. Another speaker said: "If the
King had the wealth now instead of Bishops, Abbots and
Priors, he could maintain 15 Earls, 1,500 Knights, 6,200
Esquires and have £20,000 a year for his own purposes. Where
then would be the need for crippling taxes?"[6] Yet another
with an equal aptitude for detail, reckoned that disposable
funds from the great Monasteries alone would "amount to
£214,666 per annum" or "enough to allow every township to
maintain its poor and to keep up a hundred almshouses".
Nevertheless the vociferous ones were in the minority, though
it seems likely that the Archbishop took note of those who
spoke in favour of the Bill. John Talbot was not among them.
So far as he was concerned the most useful thing that emerged
was that, following a Parliamentary vote of money, the
Exchequer was able to issue him with a tally for £4,939.6s.8d.
being some of the back pay for his men in Montgomery Castle.
As a result it was possible to increase the garrison of Goodrich
to one of 300 men-at-arms and 600 archers. [7]

The Welsh operations continued through 1410, 1411 and 1412. For John Talbot they were probably reasonably exhilarating but not so for Maud. The contrast between life in Hallamshire and in Montgomery was a stark one. The latter was a garrison fortress in an alien territory and on a war footing; while Worksop Manor, Sheffield Castle or Rufford Abbey were set in placid surroundings in an area particularly rich in culture.

Those same years were unhappy ones for Prince Henry. His father's health had steadily declined but he drove himself as hard as ever, working long hours and never stopping in one place more than two or three nights. He was incapable of government at times, and Prince Henry took control into his own hands to a considerable extent. He was aided by the Earl of Somerset, the Bishop of Winchester and Sir Thomas Beaufort. The King, in his more lucid days, strongly resented what he regarded as Prince Henry's interference, particularly as he still considered him totally irresponsible. In 1412 there was an angry scene between them, following which Prince Henry came before Parliament at Coventry to make a formal denial that he had any intention of taking the throne from his father and, full of emotion, to proclaim his affection for the King.

It seems curious that, during those same years, when Oldcastle was so openly supporting the Lollards, Prince Henry should still have reposed so much confidence in him. He was first appointed a member of a Commission to examine the defences of the lower reaches of the Thames, and then sent with, of all people, Archbishop Arundel, to help the Burgundians to re-capture Paris. Their small force covered itself with glory, but returned to find that the King had temporarily recovered his health and heartily disapproved of what Prince Henry had ordered. The year 1412 ended on a discordant note.

1413 was a momentous one and an unhappy one for John Talbot. His mother died in its early months, and it can fairly safely be assumed that she had helped to smooth the path of the somewhat difficult marriage between John and his wife, Maud. During those early months, too, there was another contretemps between the King and Prince Henry, when the Prince was accused of misappropriating public money. Prince

Henry appeared before his father in full Council and, kneeling, offered him his dagger if he sincerely doubted his love and loyalty. Desperately ill and weary though he was, the King still withheld the affection and trust which his son craved. Gone now was all the Prince's gaiety and any trace of wildness. Instead there was a grave young man, a leader of men who, if he had been able to, would have prohibited all import of wine and all drinking of alcoholic drinks in England; a man whose nickname now was "the Prince of Priests" and who, in his determination to disprove his father's opinion of him, had the single-minded aim to recover for England her lost lands in France.

In mid-December 1412 John Talbot had received the Writ, in the title of Lord Furnival, to attend Parliament at Westminster on 13th February 1413. The Convocations of Canterbury and York were convened for February 10th. At this time John Talbot, when in London, probably occupied The Furnival Inn; this was in the village of Holborn.* The Inn was still partly occupied by the Clerks of the Exchequer, an easy-going arrangement which the previous Lord Furnival had made as Lord Treasurer.

As events turned out, Parliament was never formally opened. The King was at Greenwich and those summoned to attend Parliament were told that he was too ill to move. Nobody paid very much attention to proceedings in Convocation until, suddenly, on March 6th, it became clear that a major attack was being mounted against all heretical beliefs and practices: in other words an attempt was being made to repel the threat to the power of the established Church. The proceedings began with an examination by the Lower House of a man called John Lay, from Nottingham, not far from Worksop. Under examination the man said that he had been in Oldcastle's employment until recently, and that a book found on him containing extracts from Wycliffe's heretical writings was indeed Oldcastle's property.

---

*Extract from a letter from the Guildhall Library, London, to the author, dated 6th January, 1975: "Furnival's Inn was sold to Lincoln's Inn in 1547 for £120. It was taken down in 1640 and rebuilt by Inigo Jones and later rebuilt again 1818-20, part of the site being occupied by Wood's Hotel. It is now the site of the offices of the Prudential Assurance Co."

This serious and direct implication of Oldcastle presented problems to all concerned. He was widely recognised as one of the leaders of the nobility, as a brave and loyal servant of the Crown, and as a friend of Prince Henry. If Convocation were to indict him they would have to hand him over to the Crown for punishment, by burning. But the King was for the present incapable of making decisions. Furthermore, because of Prince Henry's friendship and, as it was then thought, his sympathy for Lollardry, it seemed possible that Convocation's indictment might be set aside. This would be widely seen as a blow to the standing and authority of the Church. While these arguments went on the only person who appeared to be quite unconcerned was Oldcastle himself. He remained in the Cobham Hostel in Cheapside.   -

But on March 20th the King died. He had insisted on being brought to Westminster and, it being mid-Lent, he was carried into the Abbey to make an offering at the Shrine of the Confessor. There, in the Jerusalem Chamber, he collapsed; he died a few days later having regained consciousness for just long enough to make his peace with Prince Henry. He was buried with great magnificence in Canterbury Cathedral, and the Prince was crowned King Henry V on April 9th, 1413.

Convocation resumed its suspended sittings in May and Archbishop Arundel, probably out of tact, relinquished the Chair to the Bishop of London. Under his Chairmanship a damning case was built up against Oldcastle. In June his indictment was presented to the new King, together with evidence that he was at the centre of a Lollard conspiracy. There was evidence that this involved a general insurrection which would place the power and the wealth of the Church in the hands of the King.

Both Archbishop Arundel and the King did all they could to delay the proceedings. King Henry even took the unprecedented step of informing Convocation that he would personally endeavour to turn Oldcastle from the error of his ways and that, if he failed, he would hand him over as a heretic and, in an ominous phrase, "lend what secular aid might be needed".

All this time Oldcastle was free to come and go as he pleased, but he gave neither the Archbishop nor the King any help at all in their efforts to save his life. By August the King's patience was exhausted and, in a stormy interview with

Oldcastle at Windsor, he lost his temper and cursed and swore at his friend for his pig-headed foolishness. Without the King's permission Oldcastle left Windsor Castle and shut himself up in his Castle of Cooling in the Kent marshes. That was the signal for both the King and Convocation to act decisively.

The King issued orders to all Sheriffs to arrest unlicenced preachers and their aiders and abettors. The Archbishop issued Citatory Letters, formally summoning Oldcastle to appear before the Ecclesiastical Court at Leeds Castle to answer charges of heresy. Oldcastle still made no move and, on 23rd September the Archbishop publicly excommunicated him, citing him as a heretic.

It seems likely that both Archbishop Arundel and the King were not motivated entirely by their long-standing friendship with and their admiration for, Oldcastle. They were probably also moving cautiously because their intensive spy-system warned them that Oldcastle had very considerable public support.

The exact course of events now becomes rather confused but, on or about 23rd September, Henry personally rode into the Tower with Oldcastle and handed him over to the Governor, Sir Robert Morley. The Archbishop then went in person to offer, even at that late date, to absolve Oldcastle if he would recant. On 10th October, in the face of extraordinary ungracious and obstinate behaviour by Oldcastle, the Archbishop "with", as he said "much bitterness of heart", pronounced final sentence of excommunication on him and handed him over to the Secular Power — in other words to the Governor of the Tower. At the same time he similarly sentenced "all favourers, receivers, or defenders" of the condemned man. [8] If John Talbot felt any breath of suspicion pass over him at that moment, there is no record of it.

For some unexplained reason the Archbishop requested that Oldcastle's sentence should not be carried out for forty days, and the King agreed. The condemned man was even allowed to correspond with his friends outside the Tower and to have his fetters removed. On the night of 18th October he escaped.

The news of Oldcastle's escape was kept secret for ten days, but on the 28th October warrants were issued for his arrest and Morley was removed from his office as Governor of the Tower and imprisoned in it. He was released after a fortnight.

Meanwhile a most rigorous search was carried out for the escaped prisoner.

It is interesting to note that three years later, on 4th October, 1416, one William Parchmynor of Southfields, only a few yards from the Tower, was executed for harbouring Oldcastle between 18th October, 1413, and 8th January, 1414, although, between those dates, his house had not only been kept under constant watch but had actually been searched, as he himself was known to be an active Lollard.[9]

On November 16th, 1413, John Talbot and some six others were arrested and taken to the Tower, although no charge was preferred against them.

On December 1st Parliament met at Leicester, a location probably chosen by the King as a convenient central point in view of the short notice given by the Writs. Acting with unusual speed it appointed Sir Elias Lynet to head a Commission to arrest and interrogate persons suspected of Lollardry, and to bring them before the King. The Commission was empowered to use, and to pay liberally, agents who could secure information. There is record of at least one agent who received what was then the substantial sum of £5 for one day's work. It was no doubt due to the work of this Commission that the King was able to deal so effectively with the revolt when it did occur on the night of Tuesday, January 9th, 1414. Oldcastle and his companion in the conspiracy, Acton, were waiting for their supporters to rendezvous at the South end of Tottenham Court Road. So was King Henry with a small force of soldiers. In the darkness the conspirators walked straight into the trap and were taken prisoner, all save Oldcastle and Acton who saw the danger in time and escaped.

By dawn the King had appointed a Law Commission composed of Sir William de Roos, Sir Henry Scrope, and Sir William Crowmere, the City Mayor, to deal with all prisoners and any suspects already in custody. It began its arduous work within a matter of hours and, by the following Friday, sixty-nine had been condemned to death. On Saturday thirty-eight of them were drawn on hurdles from Newgate Prison to St. Giles Fields. There, four pairs of gallows had been hurriedly erected. Those actually convicted of heresy were cut down from the gallows while still alive and burned; the others were hanged.

On Monday, January 16th, the Commission turned its attention to the suspects in the Tower. The trials of these took considerably longer, partly because proof of guilt was more difficult to obtain, partly because the defendants had had time to prepare their defence. February passed, during which Acton was betrayed, arrested and executed as a heretic. By March 28th. most of the Commission's work had been completed and the King could issue a general pardon from which, however, the chief instigators of the rising were excluded, amongst them being John Talbot's kinsman, Thomas. [10] A week earlier, on March 22nd, King Henry issued a proclamation ordering all soldiers who owed service by virtue of fiefs or wages to report to London for service in France. This was followed immediately by a general muster of the Shire Levies; those of the five Northern Counties were to remain there as a defence against a possible Scots' attack, and the remainder were to be grouped along the Welsh Border to counter any possible danger from that quarter. During the King's absence, his younger brother, John, Duke of Bedford, would act as Regent in England.

It is not difficult to imagine John Talbot's feelings when, still imprisoned in the Tower, he learned of the preparations for the renewal of the war with France. His close association with the young King and his proven ability as a soldier in Wales would both seem to indicate that he should go with the Army to France. But it was not to be.

On March 28th Henry released him from the Tower, having appointed him King's Lieutenant in Ireland for a term of six years at a salary of £2,666.13s.4d. per annum. [11]* This, all through the middle ages, was the favourite method used for disposing of inconvenient personages [12] and Talbot can have had no illusions in that respect.

This sequence of events becomes even more inexplicable when, on July 28th, before proceeding belatedly to take up his post in Ireland, Talbot was apparently considered safe enough to be appointed a Commissioner for the trial of rebel Lollards in Shropshire. It is true that, at the time of his arrest, he had been in dispute with Arundel about the ownership of a farm at

---

*He was styled "John Talbot de Halomshire, Sire de Furnivall"

Pokmore in Shropshire.[13] His inclusion amongst those arrested may conceivably have been on that account rather than for any connection with the Lollards. Yet the dates of his arrest and release are unlikely to have been purely coincidental and the known facts undoubtedly place him under suspicion: he had been closely associated with Oldcastle for many years, and Herefordshire was recognised as a hotbed of Lollard sympathisers. It would be entirely in keeping with his extrovert, impulsive character that he should have been heard to express such sympathy in no uncertain terms, even if he would have been most unlikely to take part in any revolt against authority.

Again, he may possibly have been a party to the January revolt, but saved, as an old friend, by the King's action in having him arrested before it took place. But even if that was so and if, during his nineteen weeks of imprisonment, he somehow managed to convince Henry of his loyalty, it seems certain that from then onwards, for some reason, he forfeited the King's friendship. It was a bitter blow to such a dedicated soldier to be excluded from the campaign which culminated in the glorious victory of Agincourt.

Gilbert Talbot was not similarly affected. He was indentured for thirty men-at-arms which, on his petition dated April 29th, was reduced to twenty.[14]

Before following John Talbot to Ireland, it may perhaps be appropriate to relate the closing events of Oldcastle's life. He lived as an outlaw, mainly in the Welsh mountains, but appearing also in England now and again, or sending threatening letters to old enemies. At last, in November, 1417 his presence in lonely Broniarth near Welshpool became known to Sir Griffith Vaughan, who sent his two sons to capture the outlaw and gain the reward of 1,000 marks. Oldcastle fought valiantly, but was overcome when the wife of the farmer in whose buildings he had been hiding broke both his legs by a blow from behind with a stool. He was carried to London and to trial by the Peers in Parliament. Even there he began to preach his views and had to be curtly silenced. Inevitably, he was sentenced to the terrible death of a heretic, and went to it without showing any sign of fear.

So died the man caricatured a hundred and fifty years later

by Shakespeare. It was only when the descendants of this brave man protested, that Shakespeare changed his name from "Oldcastle" to "Falstaff".*

---

*Professor P. H. Davison, in his detailed introduction to *Henry IV, Part 1* (Penguin Books, 1968, p.29) writes:
"We can be certain that the name originally given to this character was not Falstaff but Oldcastle . . .
"Sir William Brooke, a descendant of Oldcastle's wife by a former marriage, was Lord Chamberlain for a short time in 1597. It would seem that he, or his son Sir Henry, objected to Oldcastle's being maligned. Certainly the name was changed . . ."
He also goes on to show, in his commentary, numerous places in the script where, for one reason or another, "Oldcastle" would be more appropriate than "Falstaff".
(See also *E.H.R.*, Vol XX, p.434)

CHAPTER IV

JOHN AND MAUD TALBOT landed at Dalkey, a small port near Dublin, on November 10th, 1414. [1] Dublin Castle was not then ready for them, and they occupied Finglas Castle, [2] no trace of which now exists. It was here that a son Thomas was born but died three months later. [3] Situated some four miles outside the walls of Dublin it presented something of a risk from the security point of view. His Commission as King's Lieutenant was formally read out by the Chancellor, Sir Richard Merbury, on November 30th at a Service in Holy Trinity Church, Dublin, in the presence of Archbishop Cranley, an old and infirm, but still imposing, prelate. [4]

The Irish scene which confronted the new Viceroy was as confused as ever. The loyal English, the settlers in the colony, were closely encompassed within the Pale, a nebulous boundary covering only the Counties of Dublin, Meath, Kildare and Louth. Beyond the Pale the King's Writ did not run. There was an intricate web of estates owned by what were termed the "degenerate English" who, although they had largely taken to Irish ways, were not accepted by the genuine or, as the English called them, the "Rebel Irish".

The conduct of the English settlers was governed, in theory rather than practice, by the Statutes of Kilkenny, which had been drawn up in 1366. [5] These stipulated, for instance, that English lieges were forbidden to marry the Irish or to sell to them horses, armour or, in wartime, any victuals whatsoever. They must use English names, follow English customs, speech and dress, and take no part in Irish sports such as hurley or quoits. As may be imagined, these Statutes never had much effect but it remained the duty of the Viceroy to try to enforce them. The Statutes covered, in theory, Louth, Meath, Trim, Dublin, Kildare, Carlow, Kilkenny, Wexford, Waterford and Tipperary. Beyond the Pale in the territory of the Rebel Irish, the Chieftain's rule was absolute within the terms of what was known as the "Brahon Code". This amounted to a strict standard of behaviour, violation of which carried stated and generally severe penalties. Such was the basis on which Chieftains such as Art MacMurragh, King of Leinster from

Ireland, c. 1400,

showing the areas of influence of some of the main families

1375 to 1418 and now aged about 59, ruled their territories. The "Degenerate English" had become petty princelings: typical of these were the Ormonds, the Kildares, the Desmonds and the Fitzgeralds (see Map). They managed usually to keep at bay or to buy off the Rebel Irish by arrangements such as one whereby, for many years, the Earl of Kildare paid MacMurragh 20 marks a year "for the safe-keeping of the road between Carlow and Kilkenny". They strongly resented any interference from Dublin. Nevertheless they paid their feudal dues and were not averse to calling for help against the Rebel Irish when they needed it. It was the task of the King's Lieutenant to secure the safety and pros-perity of the Settlers, and to bring the Degenerate English back within the King's suzerainty. This involved constant harassment of the aggressive Irish Chieftains.

John Talbot found Richard Merbury, his Chancellor, a staunch and much-needed ally. His home, like that of John, was in Herefordshire and his wife, Agnes, was Oldcastle's sister. Another source of support was the Mayor of Dublin, Alderman Drake. It was probably he who advised Talbot to restrain the malevolent influence of the wandering Irish Bards, who played a similar role to their counterparts in Wales. Theirs was a combination of insolent propaganda, and newsvending, with a genuine exercise of art. Just now they were jubilant, since they claimed that it was the Bard Niall O'Higgin who had "Rhymed John Stanley into his grave".[6] One of John Talbot's first actions was to "despoil many bards" and particularly one called O'Daly of Meath.[7] He also had to provide himself with an army and he called a muster of the Colonists. Few men turned out and he retaliated by imposing very heavy penalties for failure to muster. Having thus secured the services of all available liegemen with horses and arms, he organised them in bodies of 20, 100 and 1,000 and appointed Commissioners in charge who would use appropriately-sized forces to maintain law and order, and to search out and arrest criminals and outlaws.[8] In other words John Talbot organised the basis of an administrative system, where none existed, to enforce the Statutes of Kilkenny. In doing this and extending his control beyond the Pale he inevitably fell foul of the powerful "Degenerate English" Lords.

Of these the Ormond family was one of the most powerful.

James, the 3rd Earl, had spoken Gaelic and had been an accomplished Bard. His sister, Joan, had married a notable Chieftain named Taig O'Carroll, but in spite of these Irish connections he had continued to give his allegiance to the King of England and had been one of those who did so to King Richard in 1399. His son, the 4th Earl, also named James and almost a contemporary of John Talbot, had even more pronounced sympathy with the Irish. It was he who was to play a considerable part in John's life until he died, a year before John, in 1452.

When, as a mere boy of 12, Henry IV's youngest son, Prince Thomas, had been Viceroy, he and the young James Ormond had become devoted to each other, so much so that, when Prince Thomas left Ireland in 1409, James Ormond had gone with him. For five years the two young men had been inseparable, but, just before John Talbot arrived in Ireland, James Ormond had succeeded to the title as 4th Earl. He had returned to Ireland to find himself virtually ruler of the whole of Kilkenny and beyond, yet still in close liaison with Prince Thomas and thence, presumably, King Henry V. Ormond's relationship on the one hand with the English Crown and on the other with the native Irish is perhaps representative of the complications which have marked Anglo-Irish relationships over the centuries. He exemplified the "Patriotic" (or Home Rule) faction which it befell Talbot to oppose.

There was a further aggravation of the position in that John was also one of the many English "absentee landlords". Not only had he acquired lordships in Westmeath on becoming Lord Furnival but, vested for the present in Gilbert Talbot was the further lordship of Wexford.* The latter was, in fact, a matter of dispute between Gilbert and Lord Grey of Ruthyn, but those English who took little interest in their Irish lordships were held in great contempt by the so-called "Degenerate English". Whatever faults the latter may have had, they were, in the main, conscientious and enlightened landlords. Thus everywhere that John Talbot turned he found

---

*Maud Furnival, descended from Theobald de Verdun of the De Lacy line, claimed Lordship of Loch Sneedy in Westmeath, and Talbot, through William de Valence, claimed lordship of Wexford and the hereditary title of High Steward of Ireland, which is still held today.[9]

little but hostility, and, to add to his unhappiness, information kept reaching him of the successes of Henry V in
France.

Talbot began by attacking one of the strongest Irish
Chieftains. With a small but well-organised army he marched
against O'More of Leix, one of the most ancient kingships of
Ireland, and described at the time as "one of the strongest
Irish enemies of Leinster and a great chieftain of his
nation".[10] The swiftness and savagery of John's attack,
learned in the wild hills of Wales, was something new in
Ireland. He penetrated deep into Leix, "burned and destroyed
the corn, wounded and killed numbers of Irish, broke down
two Castles, delivered several English prisoners and, by
remaining in the district for six days and nights, a thing which
had not been done within living memory, he succeeded in
bringing the Chieftain to peace".[11] Also "to the great
comfort and relief of the English he repaired the bridge of
Athy" on the borders of the Irish of Leix, and erected a Tower
and fortifications for a garrison to maintain order. Further
success prompted the delighted and hard-pressed Colonists to
write from Dublin to the quite uninterested King Henry:

"Your faithful lieges were oftentimes preyed and killed
through this bridge but now your lieges, both there and
elsewhere, may suffer their cattle and goods to remain in the
fields day and night without being stolen or sustaining any
other loss, which hath not been seen here for the space of these
thirty years past. And now, upon the Monday in Whitsun
Week at Lissen-Hall in the County of Dublin, Maurice
O'Keating, Chieftain of his nation, traitor and rebel to you,
our gracious Lord, for the great fear he hath of your said
Lieutenant for himself and his nation, hath yielded up himself
to your Lieutenant without any condition with his breast
against his sword-point and a cord about his neck. Then
delivering to your said Lieutenant without ransom the English
prisoners he had taken before: to whom grace was granted by
indenture and his son given in pledge to be loyal lieges
thenceforward".[12]

One of the prisoners whose release John Talbot secured was
Thomas Fitzgerald, the rightful 5th Earl of Desmond.
Thomas was only fourteen years old when his elder brother,
John, the 4th Earl, was drowned while trying to cross the River

Suir while it was in spate. For ten years Thomas carried the Earldom but, according to the Colonists, he "fell into un-knightly ways and un-English customs". [13] He even went so far in defiance of the Statutes of Kilkenny as to make a romantic marriage with the beautiful Catherine, daughter of MacCormack, one of his vassals, in whose home he was benighted while out hunting.

Thomas' uncle James had been brought up by the O'Briens in the Anglo-Irish tradition and was far from pleased to see the Earldom "going Irish". On that pretext he "falsely and deceitfully took and detained" Thomas and usurped the Earldom. It is something of a tribute to John Talbot's sense of justice that he "bore great labours and costs"[14] about the release of Thomas. Having secured his release, however, John packed him off to fight for King Henry in France, where he died, fighting alongside Prince Thomas at Rouen, on August 20th, 1420.

With his usual dash and vigour Talbot next turned his attention to the North, and his savage attacks brought powerful Irish Chieftains such as O'Neill the Great, Macgennis, Maguire, and O'Donnell, to sue for peace. If his rule appears to us to have been unnecessarily harsh it needs to be set in the general perspective of those times.

Ireland did not come within the concept of chivalry prevalent in the rest of Europe. There, the simple convention, based on Arthurian Legend, whereby a knight had an obligation to protect the weak, had developed into an elaborate code of social behaviour. Honour and protocol had reached absurd proportions: knights bearing urgent messages in battle would delay delivering them until they had established the precedence of the messengers. King Henry V, on the way to Agincourt, inadvertently rode beyond a village which his foragers had selected as his night's quarters. He refused to turn back because he was wearing his coat-armour and chivalric tradition forbade him to retreat when thus attired. [15] Subsequently a special decree enjoined knights to shed their coat-armour when reconnoitring, so as to avoid such an awkward predicament. Such niceties of behaviour, and the conventions regarding the ransoming of prisoners, were unknown in Ireland. There the only rule was one of rough and primitive justice, with no quarter given to the loser. In these circumstances John Talbot gave as good as he got.

It was now 1416 and Maud Talbot had given birth to three children: John, Thomas and Christopher. The discomfort and roughness of life in Ireland probably did little to endear the country to Maud. Although the Viceroy's salary was stated as being 4,000 marks payable by the English Exchequer,[16] John Talbot, like the Duke of Bedford on the Scottish Border, never received any funds wherewith to pay his army. This was in no way exceptional. Even Prince Thomas had had to sell his silver and plate to make good cash which never arrived from England. So, in spite of the considerable wealth which had come to John from his father-in-law, it was not long before he was heavily in debt. His subjugation of the country was rendered fruitless when, due to failure in payment, his indentures of vassaldom were torn up, his army evaporated and the Irish resumed their normal, lawless behaviour. He had to have more money and he decided to go to England to state his case at first hand.

Talbot crossed the sea from Clontarf to England in February 1416, leaving Archbishop Cranley as Deputy Lieutenant,[17] but relying mainly on Merbury to enforce order. He found that King Henry, who had returned during the Summer to obtain reinforcements, had just left again for France. He was now laying siege to Caen, at the start of a year's campaigning which would end with almost the whole of Normandy in submission. Affairs in Ireland were of little interest to him.

Prince John of Bedford was once more Regent in England, with a Council composed of the Archbishop of Canterbury, the Bishops of Winchester and Durham, the Earl of Westmorland, Lord Grey of Ruthyn, Lord Berkeley, Lord Powis and Lord Morley. The welcome which Talbot received was hardly enthusiastic, and it was not aided by the fact that Lord Grey took great offence when John, as Lord Furnival, assumed precedence over him, and he began an action in the Courts for recovery from Gilbert Talbot of the Lordship of Wexford. Gilbert himself had gone to France with the King and was appointed Governor of Caen when it fell. The weight of Grey's lawsuit and of other family business thus fell on John's shoulders. It was not until Winter that the Court gave judgement in favour of the Talbot family but, even after long and persistent appeals by John, both Bedford and the Council refused to grant him any funds from the Exchequer. Every penny available was needed for the King's campaign in Normandy. The latter was proceeding well and he was now advancing towards Chartres. He sent Gilbert Talbot to the West of Bayeux to act as a flank guard against any attack from Brittany, while he himself took Alençon. Gilbert was surprised by a hastily raised local French cadre as he crossed the River Vire. His little force was badly cut up and he himself severely wounded. He survived the journey back to Goodrich but died there a year later. After the death of his first wife, Joan, he had married Princess Beatrix, daughter of King Joao I of Portugal and half-sister to Prince Henry the Navigator. Beatrix had borne Gilbert a daughter, named Ankaret after her Grandmother. She was still a minor when her father died.

Early in 1416 Sigismund, Emperor of the Holy Roman Empire, embarked on a round of visits to European Princes, the object of which was, he said, to unite the whole of Europe under himself in Christian unity, and to combat the militancy of Islamic rulers in the East. It was generally suspected that his real motive was the expansion of his Empire, and he was met everywhere with considerable suspicion. On April 30th he crossed the Channel to Dover after having visited Paris.

Bedford dispatched an embassy to meet the illustrious visitor and to give him a cautious welcome. It was led by Gloucester, with Salisbury, Harrington and John Talbot in attendance. They were instructed that, before allowing the Emperor to land, they must ascertain the true purpose of his visit. Led by Duke Humphrey with his sword drawn the embassy rode into the sea and boarded the Emperor's ship, demanding to know whether he came as a friend or to claim suzerainty over the land.[18] Discussion continued all day before the embassy was entirely satisfied and allowed the Emperor and his party to disembark. Bedford met them at Rochester and gave them a splendid reception. The Emperor was even allowed to attend a special session of Parliament, but his diplomatic efforts were not taken very seriously and they ceased abruptly when a French fleet attacked the Isle of Wight.

John Talbot returned to Ireland at the end of June. During his absence in England, trouble arose in Ireland. The

Patriotic Party had prevailed on Archbishop Cranley, now over 80 years old and a little senile, to convene Parliament at Trim, a small town on the edge of the Pale, north west of Dublin. Ormond, Kildare and Preston had dominated the session and had secured a vote, indicting Talbot on various counts. He was alleged to have practised excessive extortions and oppressions on both churchmen and laymen whose property he was said to have appropriated without payment. They also complained that he had plundered many people, including the Irish Bards. They delegated Cranley to take a Memorandum to the King setting out in detail this long list of complaints. Cranley was too old and ill to refuse, but some weeks elapsed while the exact text of the Memorandum was being worked out. Merbury had wisely taken no part in the proceedings and, in fact, fully expected Cranley to die before they were completed. This would have meant a suspension of Parliament and time was what Merbury needed. When at length the Memorandum was ready and had been through the processes of Parliament, Merbury pointed out that, to have any constitutional validity, it must be authenticated by the Great Seal. He, as Chancellor, refused to do that. The Patriotic Party retaliated by sending a formal complaint to the King about Merbury's conduct, as well as that of the King's Lieutenant.

Meanwhile Archbishop Cranley's health had declined and, in April, 1417 he had crossed the sea to England. He died on 25th May and was interred in his beloved New College, Oxford, of which he had been the first Warden. [19] He was a scholarly, saintly man who seems to have been rather out of place in Dublin.

Talbot felt that he had received less than adequate support from the loyal colonists, and he roundly told them so. He had received his salary, but no money from the Exchequer towards the massive payments which he had made since he became Viceroy, and he added that he did not relish becoming heavily in debt in order to protect and govern an ungrateful, incompetent, selfish community of settlers, and since they had such small regard for his services he proposed to depart out of Ireland forthwith.

This roused the colonists to action. They sent a deputation with a long and urgent letter to the King, in total contra-

diction of the Memorandum sent by the Patriotic Party. They
declared that[20] "great destruction and disease had come
upon the land" by John Talbot's recent absence, and that
worse might follow if he should now retire. They went on "We
humbly beseech your Gracious Lordship that it would please
you of your special grace to think upon your said land and in
the works of charity to have mercy and pity upon us your poor
lieges thereof who are environed on every side in war with
English rebels and Irish enemies to our continual destruction
and sorrow, and also to have your said Lieutenant, as
especially recommended to your Sovereign Lordship for the
causes aforesaid, and moreover to provide so graciously such a
sufficient payment for him that he may make himself strong
enough to resist the malice of your enemies on this side of the
sea, and his soldiers for their victuals and other things which
they took of your faithful lieges for the safety of your land
aforesaid and of your poor lieges therein. Considering that if
your forces be not here always so strongly maintained and
continued without being diminished, your Irish Enemies and
English Rebels, if they espy the contrary, although they have
put in hostages and are strongly bound (by indenture) to the
peace" (a tribute to Talbot's administrative arrangements),
"yet will they rise again unto war which is privy conquest of
your land".

The appeal then takes on a more reproving note:[21]
"Furthermore the money which your said Lieutenant doth
receive of your Gracious Lordship for the safe keeping of this
your land is so little that it doth not suffice to pay so much
unto your soldiers as is likely to maintain your wars here by a
great quantity . . ."

The Deputation returned empty-handed. John then wrote
in great detail to Bedford on July 11th, 1418 from
"Dassenhale" and again from Naas on October 10th,[22]
appealing for support—but to no avail. The King was entirely
absorbed in his French campaign, which was swallowing up all
his resources both in men and money.

On his return to Ireland Talbot had to devote his attention
once more to the southern Irish Chieftains and, in particular,
to Art MacMurragh who was now an old man but still as
defiant of the English as he had been when Richard II had
attempted to subdue him. John Talbot, profiting from the

lessons which he had learned in that campaign, used a small, highly mobile force and with this he "made divers great journeys (against MacMurragh) and strongly invaded, burned, foraged and destroyed the land, and slew numbers of their men." In the end Art had to admit defeat and, with his two sons Donnehad and Gerald, the old man sued for peace. This he did through a deputy, the Abbot of Deriske. The latter arranged a meeting at which Talbot accepted Art's submission, after which the two banqueted together. It was almost Art MacMurragh's last act before he died in his fortress at Ferns.

Talbot had been given the task of bringing the "Degenerate English" into obedience, and of securing the frontiers of the Colony. In that wild land rapid movement and incisive action were essential to success and John acquired a reputation for both which spread beyond the shores of Ireland, to France, whither so many of the Irish went to fight both for and against Henry V. It was not, however, in John Talbot's nature to harbour enmity and it seems likely that it was with a view to healing the breach between himself and Ormond that he contracted his son John to marry Ormond's daughter Elizabeth. Sadly, as became apparent within a year or two, it failed to do so and, indeed, seems to have estranged Talbot from his son. However, John now acquired some welcome support. His younger brother, Richard Talbot, Precentor of Hereford Cathedral had been consecrated Archbishop of Dublin in 1417 in succession to Archbishop Cranley. He was to hold office for 32 years, becoming Lord Justice in 1423 and Lord Chancellor of Ireland in 1424.[23] In those days Prelates and Church Dignitaries were often warriors and statesmen as well: Richard Talbot, who was also John's Deputy Lieutenant, was all three and his personality strongly influenced affairs in Ireland during his long tenure of office. During the whole of that time there was antagonism between "The Talbot Party" and "The Patriotic Party" led by Ormond and other "Degenerate English". One of Richard Talbot's first acts as Deputy Lieutenant was to arrest the Earl of Kildare, Sir Christopher Preston, and Sir John Bellair for holding illegal communication with the English rebels:[24] it was an act calculated to impress upon the Colonists that John Talbot's regime had been materially as well as spiritually reinforced.

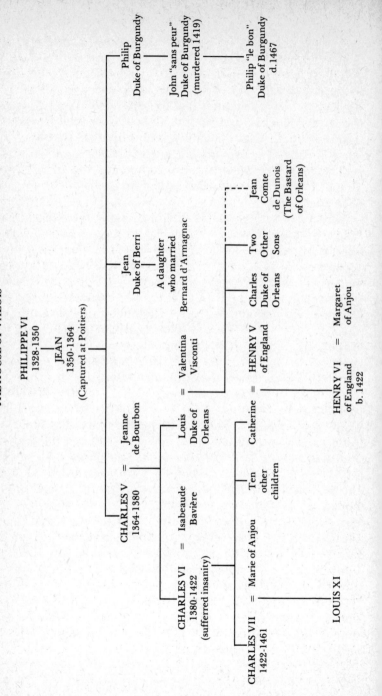

THE HOUSE OF VALOIS

PHILIPPE VI
1328-1350

JEAN
1350-1364
(Captured at Poitiers)

CHARLES V = Jeanne
1364-1380   de Bourbon

Jean
Duke of Berri

A daughter
who married
Bernard d'Armagnac

Philip
Duke of Burgundy

John "sans peur"
Duke of Burgundy
(murdered 1419)

Philip "le bon"
Duke of Burgundy
d.1467

CHARLES VI = Isabeaude
1380-1422   Bavière
(suffered insanity)

Louis
Duke of Orleans
= Valentina
Visconti

Charles
Duke of Orleans

Two
Other
Sons

Jean
Comte
de Dunois
(The Bastard
of Orleans)

CHARLES VII = Marie of Anjou
1422-1461

Ten other
children

Catherine = HENRY V
of England

HENRY VI
of England
b. 1422
= Margaret
of Anjou

LOUIS XI

CHAPTER V

EARLY IN 1419 Prince John of Bedford recalled John Talbot from Ireland and gave him "leave of absence" from his Irish Lordships for ten years.[1] In July he and Maud sailed from Howth, with three other ships carrying his retinue.

The reason for his recall lay in events which had occurred in France. These were still dominated largely by four parties. The King of France, Charles VI, and his dissolute Queen, against whom Henry V fought for what were regarded as England's domains; The Dauphin, at odds with his father and mother and holding the country south of the River Loire; and Duke John of Burgundy, an opportunist prepared to support the King or the Dauphin or King Henry according to the advantages to be gained. Of late he had lent his support to King Charles, but in June 1419 he decided to seek peace with the Dauphin. A meeting was arranged at Montereau and elaborate precautions were taken to prevent treachery. The meeting took place in the middle of the bridge over the River Gonne. The exact details have never been clear, but, as the Duke was about to kneel to the Dauphin, he was struck down and killed. His son, Philip, who now became Duke, swore vengeance for his father's murder and sent envoys at once to King Henry. The result was a new alignment of the parties. Philip of Burgundy and Henry were in a position to negotiate with King Charles and Queen Isabella, whose desire to exclude the Dauphin from any inheritance was only matched by her hopes for her daughter, Princess Catherine of Valois. For his part, the Dauphin had enlisted the support of the King of Castille, who was reported by Henry's agents to be planning a landing on the south coast of England. It was this threat which John Talbot had been recalled to meet, and Bedford had already alerted the coastal levies.

The threatened attack never materialised, and the negotiations between King Henry and King Charles went ahead. They were conducted direct with Charles during his lucid intervals, and with Queen Isabella when he was mad. By the summer of 1420 they had reached full agreement in what came to be known as the Treaty of Troyes.

Under the terms of the Treaty Charles VI of France and the Dukes of Burgundy and Brittany agreed to acknowledge Henry V as "Heir to the Crown of France" and endorsed his right to act as Regent until King Charles' death. He was then to become King of both France and England, though both Kingdoms would retain their own laws, customs and liberties. Henry's position was to be further strengthened by his marriage to Princess Catherine. In return he undertook to continue to bring under his allegiance those parts of France still loyal to the Dauphin, especially those to the North of the River Loire. Normandy and places already in his hands were to be held by him in full sovereignty.

The Treaty was signed on 21st May amid much rejoicing. It carried the seeds of much misery, many years of war, and eventually the eviction of England from the mainland of Europe. But no-one could foresee this when, with great pomp, Princess Catherine was betrothed to Henry V in the Parish Church of St. Jean, in Troyes, in June 1420. Twelve days later they were married in the same Church. King Charles had sunk into another period of insanity and the beautiful Princess was given away by her mother.

There was one small cloud in the otherwise clear sky. Bishop Beaufort of Winchester was not present, as precedence and custom demanded. He had had the presumption to accept a Cardinal's Hat without obtaining the King's permission and, in so doing, had caused deep offence.

It was characteristic of Henry V that, the very next day, he and his nobles set off to continue the siege of Melun. It proved to be a tough nut to crack, and was the scene of a fierce battle underground. Monstrelet describes it as follows:[2] "the King of England had a mine carried on with such success that it was very nearly under the walls when the besieged, having suspicions of what was intended, formed a countermine, so that a great part of the enemy's fell in and a warm engagement with lances took place . . . at which the King (of England) and Duke of Burgundy engaged two of the Dauphinois with push of pike which was afterwards continued by several knights and esquires of each party." Melun also turned out to be a most unhealthy place, where disease accounted for more than 12,000 deaths. Moreover it was a disease which persisted and continued to claim victims months after Melun fell in the

The Gatehouse, Worksop Priory (before restoration)

following November.

Back in England, John Talbot's wife Maud died during the autumn. The Manor at Worksop had been her favourite home. Her kindness to, and solicitude for, the townsfolk, together with her interest in the Priory have lived on in the liturgy of the Priory up to the present day. This was an age which saw the virtual ending of feudal rights, coupled with a quickening interest in literature and the arts, a process in which Maud played a full part.

John arranged for an exceptional and lasting memorial to her to be created at Worksop.[3] The Gatehouse of the Priory had been completed by her father just before she was born, but the two stairways to the upper room had not been enclosed. Maud had used that room for discussions with Priory officials, both in the field of art and theology: she also frequently went there in order to sit and watch the activity in the market down below. So John now arranged for the stairways which she had used so often to be enclosed in a crenellated porch and for the Arms of the Talbots and the Furnivals to be placed in separate niches over the doorway. The Gatehouse is still in use today but the niches are empty.

The Coronation of Queen Catherine took place at Westminster on February 23rd. The royal party had left Paris in mid-January and received a splendid welcome from the Londoners and the nobility, [4] who rode out over London Bridge to greet the victorious Henry and his lovely young Queen. It was the first occasion on which the King and John Talbot had come face to face since John's audience on his release from the Tower seven years earlier. Barely a month prior to Henry's return John, with the Duke of Gloucester and the Earl of Stafford, had been called upon to attend the Court Proceedings [5] relating to Oldcastle's capture: these proceedings established the right of two brothers, John and Griffith ap Griffiths (and others with them) to the reward for Oldcastle's capture. Now, as the King and John Talbot met, the ghost of Oldcastle hovered between the two men who had once been such close friends. A more substantial figure in attendance on the King was the Earl of Ormond, and as the weeks passed the enmity between Talbot and Ormond became more and more bitter. On one occasion Talbot accused Ormond of allowing traitorous behaviour on his Irish estates to go unchecked. The King coldly told John that, if he had accusations to make, he should lay them before the Court of the Earl Marshal. At the same time, possibly in an effort to make peace between the two men, he appointed John Talbot a Knight of the Garter. He then sailed for France, leaving Queen Catherine, three months' pregnant, in the care of Prince John of Bedford, who resumed his office of Protector. The King took his brother of Gloucester with him, the better to control his wildness and to keep him away from Jacqueline, Duchess of Hainault.

The Duchess, whose influence on affairs was to become considerable, was not particularly good-looking but she was gay and attractive. She was also impulsive and selfish. Her marriage to the unpleasant old Duke of Brabant had proved disastrous and, when she could stand it no longer, she fled to England to seek asylum while she petitioned the Pope for the dissolution of her marriage. She was a cousin of Duke Philip of Burgundy, and King Henry greeted her accordingly. He also, perhaps rather rashly, told his brother Gloucester to give her an official welcome. That young man's dashing good looks and pleasing manners were just what the Duchess felt she needed at such a moment and they had fallen in love. This turn of events did not please Henry, and angered Philip; the delicate alliance between the two was in jeopardy.

On December 6th, 1421, Queen Catherine gave birth to a son and King Henry's cup of happiness was full. The news was carried to him as he besieged Meaux. A week later, on December 13th, John Talbot's young niece, Ankaret, died and with her death the Talbot Barony passed to John. Thus it was under the name of Lord Furnival and Talbot that, in the early part of 1422, he formally arraigned the Earl of Ormond.

The case which he brought[6] was to the effect that the Earl was guilty of treason in that, before leaving Ireland to go to Normandy, he and his brother, Prior Thomas le Botiller of Kilmainham, purposing to harm John Talbot in his capacity of Lord of Wexford, set the (Ormond) Lordship of Oghtryn in Kildare to pay tribute, or 'black rent' as it was called, to the wife of Calvach O'Connor of Offaly being an Irish enemy: that, by that means, O'Connor, his men and those enherding unto him "often rode through those lands, despoiling, slaying and destroying the liege subjects and burning the country".

A second charge was that Ormond retained in his service William Edward, Constable of his Castle of Arklow, who "assembling O'Byrnes and other Irish Enemies to the number of 80, lay within the town of Wicklow, rose and slew John Liverpoole, Constable of the King's Castle there, smote off his head and took it to O'Byrne and then held the Castle Priests to ransom".

A third charge was that of "receiving and comforting one William Thomason, the strongest rebel and traitor in Ireland".

A fourth and final charge was that Ormond unlawfully arrested one Thomas Talbot and delivered him to hostile Irish

Kerns who took him to Calvach O'Connor who held him until John Talbot paid a ransom of £10, and then killed him. [7]

It is noticeable that all the charges relate to alleged offences against John in his private capacity. Had they been framed, as no doubt would have been possible, to allege offences against the King's Lieutenant, not only would the matter have been much more serious, but the King would have been directly involved. This would have been doubly embarrassing, because he had now appointed Ormond as Viceroy. Even as matters stood, the King was in a most difficult position: for here was an instance of the flouting of the Statutes of Kilkenny upon which his rule in Ireland depended, and by the man who was now his Viceroy there.

The King was still besieging Meaux and, even at that time, far from well. A doctor with special skill, by the name of John Swanyck, had been sent out in February to attend to him. It was thought that the disease which had ravaged the army at Melun was attacking him. Whether or not his illness had any effect on his decision in the case of Talbot versus Ormond is not known, but he ordered proceedings to be annulled and, in his Order, [8] justified his high-handed action on the grounds that both Ormond and Talbot were related to each other and to the King by blood and by marriage (see Genealogical Table, page 63). The case had aroused widespread interest and it was generally accepted that John Talbot had won a moral victory; but it did not settle their quarrel, which indeed continued until Ormond's death in 1452.

By April 1422 the King's health had seriously declined and he summoned Bedford to join him with the Queen (but not her infant son) and to bring reinforcements. Gloucester, now back in England, would take over the office of Protector. Bedford, with 300 men-at-arms and 1,000 archers, joined the King in Paris on May 30th. Meaux had fallen on May 10th, but not before the besiegers had been decimated by another terrible epidemic, which may have been either smallpox or dysentery. The King, already a sick man, seems to have caught a further infection and was a very sick man on his arrival in Paris. John Talbot, who had accompanied Bedford, went on with him to receive the surrender of Compiègne on behalf of Henry. Meanwhile the latter received a request from the Duke of Burgundy for help in the relief of Cosne, which was being

SIMPLIFIED GENEALOGICAL TABLE
SHOWING INTER-RELATION OF PLANTAGENETS, ORMONDS, TALBOTS

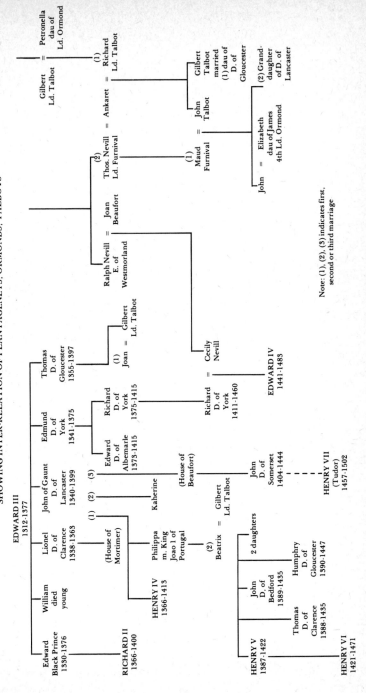

Note: (1), (2), (3) indicates first, second or third marriage

besieged by Dauphinist forces. The King replied that he would not only send help but would lead the relieving force himself.

He set out, at first on horseback, then in a litter, but at Corbeil he became too ill to continue and had himself carried back to the Bois de Vincennes. Bedford marched on, joining forces with Burgundy at Véselay on the River Yonne on August 4th. The combined armies were formidable and they reached Cosne on August 11th. There was no sign of the Dauphin and his besieging army. The report that Henry V himself was advancing against him had proved sufficient for the Dauphin to decide that discretion was preferable to valour, and he had retreated to his base at Bourges.

The unpredictable behaviour of the Duke of Burgundy now made itself apparent. Instead of seizing the opportunity of recapturing La Charité-sur-Loire, or even of inflicting a lasting defeat on the Dauphinist army in retreat, he took an extraordinary decision. After the minimum consultation with Bedford he marched his army away to Troyes, where he disbanded it. Bedford then gave orders for the English army to return to Paris. But, almost immediately news reached them that the King was dying. The army commanders hastened to the King's bedside at Vincennes. They arrived there on August 20th.

The King's courage was magnificent. He was in intolerable pain but his brain worked as coolly and lucidly as ever while, for ten agonising days, they watched him slowly dying. During that time he lectured Bedford and the rest as to how affairs should be conducted after his death. Yet, such was the stress of those days, that those present could only vaguely recall the instructions which he had given them.

Bedford was to be Regent for the infant King Henry VI, whom his father would now never see. There was mention of Humphrey of Gloucester as Protector in England, or perhaps it was only while Bedford was absent. It did not seem to matter much then, as the King lay dying. There were strict injunctions to fulfil the conditions of the Treaty of Troyes: to conquer all France north of the River Loire and to retain Normandy at all costs. There was, so far as they could recall afterwards, no detailed mention of affairs in England or Ireland. But most of them had grown up with Henry, hunted with him, fought alongside him and loved him for his single-mindedness and his courage, and they agreed later that they could not concentrate on what he was saying. Even Salisbury, whose father had been executed for his part in the insurrection against Henry, had tears in his eyes[9] as he watched him dying.

CHAPTER VI

HENRY V WAS DEAD, and for many people something of England died with him;[1] some elements of the age of chivalry. A new era opened in which fear, mistrust, greed and self-interest became widespread in a way that had not been seen since Henry Bolingbroke took the throne. John of Bedford, the most honourable and unselfish of men, was left to face a formidable task: he had to exercise authority without the position and prestige of kingship, or the military reputation which his dead brothers, Henry, and Prince Thomas of Clarence, had enjoyed.

In England, his other brother Humphrey of Gloucester was erratic and ambitious, and a bitter jealousy existed between him and the equally ambitious Cardinal Beaufort, Bishop of Winchester. The English garrisons in France were spread over an area almost as large as England south of a line from the Wash to the Severn Estuary. They numbered some 15,000 combatant soldiers, and it was clear to the English Commanders that, if northern France was to be held, then the Burgundian Alliance must be maintained. Yet even that was precarious; Philip of Burgundy himself could not be trusted. Then aged 24, he was selfish and ambitious and was reputed to have at least thirty mistresses and a corresponding number of bastards.

Charles VI died on October 22nd, and France was restive under the hand of the English Regent. Bedford had tried to persuade Duke Philip to become Regent but he had refused; so Bedford, feeling that authority must be in evidence at the French King's funeral, had taken the place of precedence, and had had the French Sword of Justice carried before him as symbol of it. Parisians, seeing this, realised for the first time the full significance of the Treaty of Troyes, and they did not like it. The administration of Normandy was divided into seven Baillies which, in turn, were subdivided into Viscomtès which were administered by Norman officials. Even they felt that they owed little allegiance to an English Regent. All the same Bedford was encouraged by the supine inaction of the Dauphin. On his father's death he had issued a proclamation

as King Charles VII, but had taken no steps to assert his claim
to the Throne and had continued to live in luxury at Bourges.

It was thus the English rather than the French aspect of his
Regency which at first exercised Bedford. He called a meeting
of Parliament at Westminster for 5th November, 1422 and,
pending the election of a representative Council of State,
appointed a temporary Council to act with and for him. It was
as a member of this Council that, together with about eleven
others and led by Simon Guernstede, the Keeper of the
Chancery Rolls, John Talbot was present at the first ceremony
performed in the presence of the infant Henry VI. [2] On the
afternoon of September 28th, the Delegation trooped into
Windsor Castle, led by the Chancellor, the Bishop of Durham,
carrying the Great Seal on a red cushion. They were ushered
into the Great Hall. There the widowed Queen Catherine,
holding the infant King in her arms, accepted the Great Seal
on his behalf and then each member of the Council made the
oath of allegiance to him. They noticed that the baby slept
throughout the proceedings.

On October 3rd the Council formally empowered John
Talbot, Lord Ferrers and William Talbot, a cousin of John's,
to maintain order on the Welsh Marches including the
Counties of Shropshire, Hereford, Worcester and Gloucester.
It would almost appear from the wording of the document [3]
that riots were anticipated. However, they did not occur.

When Parliament met, Bedford contented himself with
settling the formalities arising out of the Sovereign's death, the
infancy of his son, and the consequent Regency. Parliament
was prepared to accept his nominations to the Council of
State, the full membership of which consisted of the
Archbishop of Canterbury, the Bishops of Winchester,
Durham, Norwich, Exeter, Worcester, Lincoln and Rochester,
the Dukes of Gloucester and Exeter, the Earls of Warwick,
Norfolk and Northumberland, Lords Ferrers, Botreaux,
Clinton, Dudley, Fitzhugh, Poynings, Berkeley, Cromwell and
Talbot. [4] Ormond, who had been a member of the
temporary Council and who had been amongst those who went
to Windsor Castle, was not elected to the permanent Council.
Bedford had ordered him to take up his appointment in
Dublin. Before he did so, on a wet and blustery night in
January, he and his men set on John Talbot as he made his way

home to the Talbot Inn in Whitechapel. His men easily beat off the attack and he laid a formal complaint against Ormond the following day. The case was heard in the Court of Chancery on 11th February and they were each ordered, under pain of 10,000 marks fine, to give an undertaking "not to do or procure hurt or harm" to each other.

The exact terms under which Gloucester was to exercise authority in England exercised both Bedford himself and the Council. Gloucester's unreliability and lack of judgment were recognised by everyone except himself. At that time, too, his obsession with Jacqueline of Hainault was embarrassing. The Council felt strongly that any powers which he might be given must be strictly limited. But Gloucester saw matters quite differently. According to him his brother had, on his death-bed, appointed Bedford Regent of France and himself, Humphrey, Regent of England. As such he claimed that he had inherited full and unfettered authority.

Unfortunately, none of those who had been present during Henry V's last hours could recall exactly what he had said in respect of the Regency. Their recollection was that he had said that Bedford should be Regent, meaning Regent in both England and France, but that, while Bedford was engaged in the wars in France, Gloucester should be Regent in England. They were, however, far from unanimous about it. They were adamant that, whatever the dying Henry might have said, the English Regency only held its powers by virtue of the decree of Parliament, of whom they, as Members of the Council of State, were the executive spokesmen. Gloucester would have to govern England according to the policy laid down by them. Gloucester eventually had to accept that position, though he did so with the worst possible grace and with bad blood between himself and Bishop Beaufort, the Council's Chairman. It constituted an important advance towards modern Parliamentary supremacy, but it was also the first hint of the internal struggle for power which was to end in Civil War forty years later.

With the Regency question settled, Bedford returned to France in the early weeks of 1423. During that summer he drove the Dauphinists out of Picardy, while Salisbury invested Mont Aiguillon, fifty miles south east of Paris, thus dominating Brie and Champagne. Bedford was equally successful on the diplomatic front even if the foundations were somewhat shaky. He succeeded in getting Duke Philip of Burgundy and Duke John of Brittany to meet him at Amiens and on 13th April they concluded an Agreement.

In order to ensure that Duke John knew what he was signing, Bedford made him read its terms aloud. They were explicitly to the effect that the three Princes would work together to recover the whole of France for Henry VI. Yet on 18th April Duke Philip and Duke John signed a secret treaty to the effect that, if either of them became reconciled to the Dauphin, they would remain friendly together. At the same time Bedford married Anne of Burgundy, Duke Philip's nineteen year old sister. This was primarily a political marriage and, in truth, Anne was no great beauty. She had heavy Flemish features and limbs, fair hair and pale blue eyes. But her looks were deceptive and her character direct and attractive. She and Bedford were the most devoted husband and wife and his wedding present to her, a Book of Hours, was a beautiful and appropriate work of art. They were married on Ascension Day in that same Church of St. Jean in Troyes where Henry V had married Catherine of Valois just three years previously. Only the Nave of the original Church still survives.

Talbot sailed from Sandwich in April 1423 to join Bedford with a contingent of 2,700 men. He had had his muster ready in mid-February but had refused to move them until he had been paid some of the arrears due to him. The operation involved the use of 7 barges, 37 cargo vessels and 6 coggeships (rowing vessels) with a total tonnage of 2,538 tonnes and a crew of 534 men. The cost of the operation was £552.5s.3d. [6] During the year he assisted Bedford and Salisbury in operations which resulted in the surrender of Le Crotoy and Mont Aiguillon, extending still further England's hold on Northern France.

By now Bedford had assumed his full status. At the age of 34 he was tall and more heavily built than his older brother, whose mantle he had now assumed. He and John Talbot were curiously similar, and contemporary chroniclers remark about both men that their sense of justice and right won them many friends, not the least being Duke John of Luxemburg. Both of them were equally popular with the villagers and townsfolk, but the lesser nobility hated them and, so far as the French were concerned, many went into exile rather than live under their rule. Arthur de Richemont was such a one. He was a younger brother of the Duke of Brittany, an ally of some importance to England. De Richemont managed to offend all with whom he came in contact. He had been taken prisoner by Henry V at Agincourt and had subsequently broken his parole (an unforgivable offence under the rules of chivalry), by not surrendering himself at Michaelmas 1422 nor paying his ransom. However, in the interests of good relations with Brittany, both King Henry and Bedford had overlooked it. Marauding parties had lately been particularly active around Paris and Count Arthur approached Bedford in his head-quarters at Rouen with the request that he should be given command of an Anglo-Breton force to police the area. Bedford made no attempt to keep the contempt out of his voice as he refused and Count Arthur made some sneering reply. Without another word Bedford's fist shot out and the Breton fell. For a moment it looked to those around as if he would draw his sword on the Regent.[7] Instead he turned and left the Chamber and, within an hour, had left the City on the road to Bourges. The alliance with Brittany was once again in disarray.

It was about this time that John Talbot began to think about re-marriage. He was forty years old but, in spite of his advanced age as it was then considered, he had fallin love with Margaret Beauchamp, Warwick's only daughter. She was then twenty years old and everything that Maud had not been: gay, impetuous, hot-tempered and strong-willed. According to Mr. James Smyth, Archivist of the Warwick MSS, she was never free of law suits from the age of 21 until her death in 1467. She was also something of a Martinet according to the inscription on her tomb in old St. Paul's which read:[8] "Her reson was 'Til deth departe'. This lady to the honour of god made a decre in her hows nother own childre owt set that what ever person blasphamyd our Lord by unlawful swerying he should lak that day ale wyn and chochyn (?cooking) and only have but bred and watre".

John Talbot and Margaret Beauchamp were married in Paris in July 1424 and John gave his bride an illuminated Prayer Book. Its cover depicts the two of them kneeling at the feet of the Virgin Mother to receive her blessing. Their marriage was indeed blessed.

In the summer of 1423 the Dauphin had at last spurred himself into action, possibly as a result of the arrival at Bourges of a strong contingent from Scotland. The Scots, anxious as ever to embarrass the English, considered that they could best do so by bolstering the poor morale of the Dauphinists and they sent their Marshal, Sir John Stewart of Darnley, to command the army. The Dauphin raised additional men and dispatched this formidable force eastwards into Burgundy with orders to capture Cravant on the River Yonne. By this move he hoped to re-establish communications with his supporters in Picardy and Champagne and to pose a threat to Paris and, at the same time confront his army with Burgundian forces rather than the redoubtable English archers. This was the first real test of Bedford's generalship and of his alliance with Burgundy. His reaction was prompt and vigorous. He ordered Salisbury to march at once to the relief of Cravant, while the Dowager Duchess of Burgundy also raised a small force. The two contingents met at Auxerre on July 29th and Salisbury convened a conference in the Cathedral. It is not clear whether Waurin was actually present but he records its decisions in great detail as also does Monstrelet. [9] The English professional soldiers did not disguise their contempt for the prowess of their Burgundian companions-in-arms, and were, as a result, notoriously difficult and touchy as allies. The Chroniclers underline this. According to them both, it was agreed that the two contingents should form one indivisible force under Salisbury's command and meticulous attention was paid to the details of their complete and harmonious integration. Two Marshals were appointed to control the movements and discipline of the troops; one was to be English and the other Burgundian. Each soldier was to carry on his person food for two days. The townspeople of Auxerre were to provide provisions for the whole army (not merely the Burgundian contingents, as the latter might have expected, while it was in their vicinity).

Each archer was to provide himself with a stake pointed at both ends to plant in the ground to his front. (This was normal English practice.)

Each soldier was to keep his exact station in the ranks,

penalty for falling out being a flogging.

A party of 60 English and 60 Burgundians was to go forward as scouts.

On approaching the enemy everyone on horseback was to dismount and all horses were to be led half a mile to the rear.

Finally, no prisoners were to be taken until the issue of the battle had been decided.

The need for the exact provisions of this mutual operations order, as it might be called, indicates both the care for detail evinced by Bedford and his subordinates, and the precarious relationship between the English and Burgundian soldiers. At 10 o'clock the next morning the whole army marched out of Auxerre with, as the Chronicler Waurin relates, "much brotherly love". In the battle which followed, at Cravant, the Dauphinist army was completely anihilated. The Lombards and the Spaniards were the first to fly, while the Scots stood their ground and suffered very heavy casualties. Sir John Stewart was not only taken prisoner but lost an eye in the fighting. In that one major battle the Dauphin's offensive had been crushed, and contingents under Suffolk, Duke John of Luxemburg and a certain Captain Glasdale, who came to fame a few years later, penetrated as far as Macon, a hundred miles inside Dauphinist territory.

In 1424 Bedford repeated his success when his army of some 8,000 men routed one of 15,000 in the epic battle of Verneuil, on August 17th 1424. Waurin, who was present both there and at Agincourt, says that Verneuil was the tougher battle of the two. Certainly the members of a large contingent of Scots were thirsting to avenge their defeat at Cravant and fought fiercely even when, in the end, they were taken in the rear by Bedford's men-at-arms. He had shown his disregard for the disparity in numbers when, prior to the battle, he had actually sent L'Isle Adam away with his Burgundians to resume their clearing-up operations in Picardy and had left Warwick and John Talbot in Paris. He wrote jubilantly to Sir Thomas Rempston,[10] another able commander who was with Warwick, and also to John of Luxemburg saying that, by the count of the heralds, 7,262 of the enemy had been killed while the English had only lost about 1,000 men.[11]

In the weeks which followed Verneuil the prospects for the English cause in France seemed brighter than they had ever been. The opposition had melted away and there was nothing to prevent Bedford marching on Bourges. Such a move might possibly have ended the war but it is more likely that the Dauphin would have fallen back still further south and set up another capital there. Whatever Bedford may have thought on that score, he held to his original plan to gain complete control of Anjou and Maine and to attempt the capture of Mont St. Michel.

But now he sustained two severe setbacks. Philip of Burgundy was in Paris for the wedding of his Maître d'Hotel, Jean de la Trémoile, at which Lord and Lady Salisbury were also present. Duke Philip was no puritan and was accustomed to getting what he wanted. He blatantly sought the favours of the beautiful Lady Salisbury. Salisbury was so furious that he swore that he would never again fight alongside Philip and, worse still, took himself off to England there to demonstrate his antipathy to Burgundy by assisting Gloucester in his efforts to help Jacqueline of Hainault regain her lost provinces. Philip challenged Gloucester to a duel.

The brief Anglo-Burgundian alliance now seemed ended and indeed it almost looked as if English and Burgundian soldiers would soon be fighting each other. Luckily Gloucester did not receive the welcome from the Low Countries which Jacqueline had led him to expect, and meanwhile his ardour for her had cooled rapidly in favour, first of the wife of one of her equerries and then of Eleanor Cobham, Oldcastle's widow, a woman of great beauty and courage. So, when Duke Philip challenged Gloucester to a duel, Bedford and his wife, Anne, were able to act as arbiters between the two. The Anglo-Burgundian alliance was shaken but it survived.

Bedford sent John Talbot back to England to strengthen his representation on the Council of State in its dealings with Gloucester, and John and Margaret also took an opportunity of crossing to Ireland in January 1425. They landed at Howth and it so happened that, just as they arrived, the Viceroy, the Earl of March, caught the plague and died. His pro-Irish policy, following as it did that of Ormond, had reduced the colonists almost to despair in spite of all that Richard Talbot could do on their behalf. He had even refused to recognise March's Deputy, the pro-Irish Bishop of Meath, but he had been over-ruled. When March died the delighted colonists immediately asked John Talbot to act as Viceroy until a new appointment was made. He accepted, and set about the job with his usual vigour.

He found some of the Northern chieftains actually resident in March's Castle at Trim. He took them prisoner and secured ransoms from the Irish before releasing them. He relieved the pressure on the colonists in Meath and Westmeath, and forced Donagh, Chief of the O'Byrnes, to covenant to protect the loyal English in John's Lordship of Wexford. Donagh also gave him "three good horses and three good hackneys". [12] During those same months John Talbot made over various parts of his Irish Lordships to his two sons by his first wife Maud. It was about this time, too, that he enfieffed the Manor of Painswick to Margaret. The ravages of the plague in England had caused an acute shortage of labour and, as the country gradually emerged from the feudal system, the new one of leasehold land tenure was causing trouble. There were many problems arising out of rent collection, repairs, grazing and gleaning rights, and other matters to be settled. John and Margaret Talbot were pioneers in dealing with this situation.

During the summer of 1425 Gloucester was causing fresh trouble, and John's presence was again required in the Council of State. The quarrel between Gloucester and Beaufort came to a head on October 29th, in a slightly ludicrous contest for control of the City of London. Gloucester sent for John Coventry, the newly elected Lord Mayor, and the City Aldermen, and besought them to "keep well the city that night and make good watch", [13] as he had heard that Beaufort intended to capture the infant Henry VI and then the Tower of London, in a bid for power. Barricades were placed on the south end of London Bridge and, sure enough, between 9.0 o'clock and 11 o'clock that night Beaufort approached with some armed men and removed the barricades. When challenged he maintained that he was doing so to prevent Gloucester taking possession of the City. Londoners rallied to Gloucester and, for the next twenty-four hours, two bodies of armed men faced each other in suspense. Meanwhile Archbishop Chichele and Prince Peter of Portugal rode furiously backwards and forwards across the bridge, mediating between the two leaders. Eventually the two armed bands dispersed, but the dispute between Gloucester and Beaufort continued with increasing bitterness.

The incident seriously worried Archbishop Chichele, who sent an urgent message to Bedford saying that he must return to England at once if civil war was to be avoided. The message reached Bedford the same day as he heard that Arthur de Richemont had persuaded his brother to defect from the Triple Alliance and go over to the Dauphin. However, the quarrel with Burgundy had been sufficiently patched up for Bedford to leave the Duke in charge as President of the Council and, leaving Salisbury, Suffolk and Warwick in command of military operations in Normandy, he and Anne left Paris for London on December 1st with an escort of 500 men. It was as well that they took such a large escort, for they were ambushed near Amiens by a notorious bandit named Fremanville; but they escaped without harm. [14]

They landed at Sandwich on December 20th, 1425, and found Beaufort waiting for them. He wanted to get in first before Gloucester gave his version of recent events. He also wanted to make a formal complaint that Gloucester had incited a mob to attack Winchester House in Southwark. He did, however, admit that it contained a garrison of archers recruited from Cheshire and Lancashire who would therefore be regarded by Londoners as foreigners and, as such, subject to attack.

Bedford took the whole situation very calmly, although the dispute between the two men had completely upset his planned operations in France. He reminded Beaufort that his own presence in England automatically deprived Gloucester of any official position. Besides, Christmas was approaching when there should be good will all round. Bedford, and especially Anne, were intensely fervent in their religion, and Christmas was of great importance to them. They spent it happily at Eltham Palace. There, for the first time, Bedford met the baby King, a shy, solemn, fair-haired little child just four years old, and gave him, as a Christmas present, a gold ring set with a ruby. [15]

Bedford had called a Council Meeting for January 29th, 1426, but had asked the Members of it to accompany him, as was their duty, when he made his official entry into the City on January 10th. The crowd gave him an enthusiastic welcome but, at one point, booed Beaufort riding a few yards behind him. Bedford made it completely clear that his sympathies were, if anything, on the side of Beaufort. [16]

Gloucester was not present, and when the Council met he sent a message to the effect that he refused to attend it so long as Beaufort was there. Beaufort made his report, and Bedford then asked him to leave the Chamber while the matter was discussed. It was obvious that no progress could be made until both the main protagonists could be persuaded to be present, and it was agreed that a deputation should go to see Gloucester and urge him to attend the next Meeting of the Council, which would be held at Northampton on February 13th, 1426; Archbishop Chichele, Lord Stafford, Lord Cromwell, Sir John Cornwall and John Talbot were chosen for this task. [17]

Gloucester was convinced that, with the Londoners behind him, he was in a strong position and he replied to the Deputation by making two impossible demands: that he alone and not Beaufort should be heard by the Council, and that, before the Meeting, Beaufort should resign from the Chancellorship. The Deputation replied that, to force the resignation of the Chancellor in such a way would be an attack on the Royal Prerogative, and in the end, neither Gloucester nor Beaufort attended the Council Meeting on February 13th.

Parliament then met at Leicester on February 18th. It was known as the "Parliament of Bats" since, forbidden to carry arms, members carried clubs and staves. When these, too, were banned so tense was the atmosphere that they hid stones in their clothes. For ten days only routine business was carried out, and then, on February 28th, the Commons sent a petition to the Lords asking them to heal the divisions which existed between certain eminent personages. Bedford was in a very difficult position. Gloucester's nature was extremely temperamental, yet he was third in succession to the throne, occupied now by a sickly child; in Bedford's absence in France, moreover, much depended on Gloucester's support in England: his pride must not be wounded. But Bedford saw clearly the need for ultimate power being in the hands of the Council of State.

Beaufort also presented a problem. Not only was the Crown heavily in debt to him through countless loans secured on the Customs of various Ports, and even on Royal jewelry and plate, but he was also cleverer and more able than his rival.

Bedford was tactful but firm, and eventually it was arranged that the matter should be decided by a Commission of Peers. They met on March 7th, and the hearing went on for four days. They ordered Beaufort to declare, in the presence of Bedford, the Lords and the Commons, that he had always borne true allegiance to the Sovereigns of the House of Lancaster. Beaufort accepted defeat. He made the required declaration to a packed house of Lords and Commons, whereupon Bedford declared him to be a true and loyal subject. Beaufort then declared his peace with Gloucester. "I never imagined or purposed anything", he said, "that might be hindering or prejudice to your person, honour or estate", and on that the two men shook hands. [20]

Two days later Beaufort delivered up the Great Seal of the Chancellorship to Bedford, and John Kemp, Bishop of London, was appointed Chancellor in his place. Beaufort then tactfully left the country, ostensibly on a pilgrimage.

Gloucester, of course, considered with some justification that he had defeated all the other parties concerned: Bedford, Beaufort and the Council of State. But he underestimated his brother. Bedford called a Meeting of the Council on November 24th, 1426 at which he produced draft Rules defining the Council's power and thus curbing those of the Protector. Gloucester was not at the Meeting, which unanimously approved the draft. Gloucester was also absent when the Council met again on January 28th, 1427. Bishop Kemp read out the Rules which defined the powers of the Council as being "the supreme authority of the Realm, the executive of which standeth as now in the King's Lords assembled either by authority of Parliament or in the King's Council". [21] Thus, when Parliament was not in session, full authority lay with the Council and not with the Protector. The step taken in 1422 towards Parliamentary supremacy was now consolidated.

Bedford declared his acceptance, as well he might, having drafted the Rule, and he suggested that, as Gloucester was not present, the Chancellor should take the document to him, explain its significance, and ask him, too, to declare his acceptance of it. Gloucester was furious, but he could hardly refuse to accept what Bedford had already agreed to. Nevertheless he regarded it as bitterly humiliating and never forgave either Bedford or the other members of the Council for inflicting it upon him.

Bedford was much relieved that the situation had now been resolved, and delighted that he and Anne could take a holiday. It was the only real respite of their married life.

CHAPTER VII

ON MARCH 19th, 1427 Bedford and John Talbot, with their wives, sailed for France from Sandwich. Talbot had with him 300 men-at-arms, 900 archers and some powerful artillery, the latter in the charge of four Master Artillerymen. [1] When they landed at Calais Beaufort was waiting with two Papal Legates. On March 25th, in St. Mary's Church, Bedford placed the Cardinal's Hat on his uncle's head and the Papal Bull was read declaring him to be a Cardinal. [2] In effect he was granted official forgiveness for having originally accepted the Cardinal's Hat without permission in 1420.

During Bedford's preoccupation with affairs in England matters had not gone well in France. In January 1426, a day or two before leaving for England, Bedford had heard of the Duke of Brittany's defection to the Dauphin and had formally declared war on him. His brother de Richemont had taken the unsuspecting English garrison of Pontorson by surprise, captured the town and put every English man, woman and child to death. One of Bedford's last orders before he left for England was to Sir Thomas Rempston, who had a force of only some 500 men, to march on Rennes and make the Duke of Brittany regret his change of heart. Rempston was just the man for this, being young and resourceful. However, on approaching Rennes, he heard that de Richemont (who now styled himself Constable of France) was moving on Fougères with a force of 10,000 men and some artillery. Rempston thereupon returned to Beuvron, on the Normandy border, midway between Avranches and Fougères. In making this move he fully expected that Suffolk, who was at Fougères, would come to his aid. But, when de Richemont attacked Beuvron, Suffolk made no immediate move; in fact the young man (he was 26 years old) was so slow in taking action that he did not arrive at Beuvron until two days after the battle.

However, while de Richemont's guns were breaching the walls of Beuvron, Rempston's men crept out through a sally port, got round behind the enemy and attacked them in the dark with loud cries of "Salisbury! Saint George!". [3] At the same time the garrison of Beuvron re-doubled their fire from

79

the walls. The French, imagining that Salisbury had arrived with a relieving force, fled. Rempston's men attacked the French camp and created such panic there that the whole army dribbled away and did not stop until they reached their base at Fougères. In was victories such as this which gave the English confidence in their ability to defeat the French no matter what the numerical odds against them.

In the face of his brother's defeat at Beuvron, the Duke of Brittany asked for a three months' truce. Suffolk agreed and, by the summer of 1427, Duke John had recognised Henry VI as King of France. In a little over eighteen months his allegiance had come full circle.

In June 1427 Suffolk joined forces with Warwick and advanced into Eastern France where, on 1st July, they laid siege to Montargis, 60 miles south east of Paris and 40 miles east of Orleans. There, he was to come face to face with two of the Dauphin's most able commanders: La Hire, who had been recently captured and ransomed, and the young Count of Dunois. These two fell upon Suffolk's besieging army, captured his brother and relieved the town. The English retreated, leaving behind most of their guns and siege equipment. The French were jubilant over what they regarded as a significant victory. [4] It was certainly a major disaster for Bedford who was, in any case, short of soldiers. It had, for some time, been a severe handicap to operations in France that Burgundy, who had not openly broken with the English, had nevertheless withdrawn his army into the Low Countries to meet the threat posed by Jacqueline of Hainault. The only Burgundian commander who still kept the field with Bedford was Duke John of Luxemburg, whose men had to be paid as mercenaries.

Duke Philip's Court was now one of great culture and elegance. Painters such as Jan van Eyck and Roger van de Weyden were in his patronage; also men of letters such as Chastillain, Olivier de la Marche, and Gerson, probably the foremost theologian of his time.

In July, 1427, Gloucester succeeded in persuading those Members of the Council left in England to grant him 5,000 marks to spend on raising soldiers for Jacqueline. To do the Council justice, they did at least stipulate that the troops must be used only in Holland, and for purely defensive purposes;

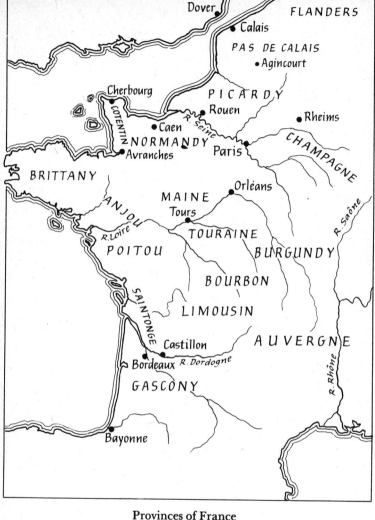

Provinces of France

but it was a foolish step for Gloucester to take. Bedford wrote to his brother imploring him to abandon Jacqueline's cause once and for all. This advice came at the right moment, as Gloucester had ceased to live with Jacqueline (to whom he was supposedly married) and was now living with Eleanor Cobham. Bedford sent Salisbury over to England to impress all this on Gloucester, and to bring back more soldiers. His

Northern France

efforts were successful. The expedition to Holland never took place, Gloucester married Eleanor Cobham, his so-called previous marriage having been declared void in the eyes of the Church; and rather surprisingly Jacqueline made her peace with Duke Philip. Once again Bedford had saved the fragile structure of alliances on which operations in France depended, and once again he could give those operations his individual attention.

His first step was to appoint John Talbot Governor of Anjou and Maine, with full power to subjugate the area. Talbot brought to this task the same energy which he had employed first in Wales and then in Ireland. By appearing suddenly where he was least expected he instilled fear into the hearts of the populace, but he tempered his rule with a rough justice which won him their respect. It was here that he acquired the soubriquet of "the English Achilles".

A typical operation occurred in March 1428. Suffolk, who was in charge of operations around the Maine border, had his headquarters at Le Mans. John Talbot with Sir John Fastolf was at Alençon, 30 miles to the north, collecting and training a force for a summer campaign against Laval, fifty miles to the south west.

In the evening of March 26th, when Talbot was on the point of retiring to bed, an exhausted messenger was brought to him. His name was Matthew Gough, and he had been sent by Suffolk. That morning at sunrise La Hire had attacked Le Mans. There had been treachery from inside and the gates had been opened and the sentries killed. Suffolk and his bodyguard had just managed to take refuge in the Keep. It was from there that Gough had managed to escape. John Talbot reacted quickly. He picked three hundred of his best mounted archers and, galloping through the darkness, they were in the hamlet of Guyerche, two miles from Le Mans in the early hours. He positioned his men in the woods a mile north of the town an hour before dawn, having sent Gough forward as a scout. To quote Hall's account: "Gough so well sped that prively in the night he came into the Castle where he knew that the Frenchmen . . . began to wax wanton as though their enemies could do them no damage (being shut up in the castle). When Gough had eaten a little bread and drunk a cup of wine to comfort his stomach he prively returned again" to meet Talbot at the rendezvous. As a result of his daring he was able to report that he had got close enough to La Hire's sentries to ascertain that they had no inkling at all that any enemy was within miles of them. While it was still dark Talbot sent Scales, one of his able lieutenants, with a small party to attack the North gate, while he simultaneously attacked the unsuspecting sentries on the South gate, the direction from which he was least likely to come. La Hire was taken completely by surprise, but managed to escape. His force was cut to pieces, many men leaping from the walls clad only in their shirts.

After Le Mans had been liberated, Suffolk summarily tried and excuted those who had helped the French. The fact that he had yet again suffered a reverse did nothing to enhance his reputation in Bedford's eyes.

Within a few weeks John Talbot considered himself strong

enough to attack Laval. Once again he achieved surprise by a night approach, and the town fell with little loss of life. Talbot was then able to tell Bedford that Maine lay open to him.

In July 1428 Bedford summoned all his commanders to Paris for a major discussion on policy.[6] Salisbury had met with great opposition when he had tried to raise men and money in England the previous year. There was no doubt at all that the war in France had lost all the glamour and popularity with which Henry V had endowed it. Indeed it had become highly unpopular, as had the high taxes required to pay for it. Manpower, already depleted by years of war and plague, could ill be spared from the English farms. Nevertheless Salisbury had managed to raise 450 men-at-arms, 2,250 archers, 10 miners, 70 carpenters, masons, bowmakers and wheelwrights, and a few other craftsmen: a self-sufficient force in itself.[7] Waurin adds that they were "well chosen and experienced in arms".[8] The English Exchequer had contributed £24,000 and the French Estates 180,000 Livres (Bedford had asked for 200,000). Bedford estimated that, by collecting contingents from outlying garrisons, he could muster an army of 5,000 men, with supporting manpower. His problem, as he put it to his commanders, was to decide upon the next step to be taken.

Salisbury, Warwick, Suffolk and Talbot were present, and in the discussions which followed two schools of thought emerged. The first considered that a wide sweep should be made, through Maine and Anjou, linking up eventually with the ardently pro-English people of Gascony. The Dauphin would thus find himself almost entirely encircled, his only ports would be on the Mediterranean coast, and Scottish help would be much less easy to obtain.

The other school favoured a direct attack on Bourges as being both the most sound from a tactical point of view, and, almost as important, less costly in men and money. It would, however, entail the capture of Orleans sixty miles from Paris and about the same distance from Bourges.

Most of the commanders preferred this second plan, but Bedford himself strongly opposed it.[9] It was not, he said, that the plan itself was unsound but that Orleans was part of the domain of Charles of Orleans, who had been a prisoner in England since Agincourt. Bedford felt that it was contrary to the strict code of chivalry to attack the lands of someone who was his prisoner. However, he was in a minority of one and he very reluctantly gave the second plan his approval. He did, however, say that he himself could not take command of the operation, which he would therefore entrust to Salisbury. He wished John Talbot to remain as Governor of Maine and Anjou, with his base at Falaise, a town of which he was Captain and with which he and Margaret were by now very closely associated.

Following the agreed plan Salisbury quickly captured some forty towns either directly on his route to, or affecting the defence of, Orleans. Included among them were Meung and Beaugency down-river, and Jargeaux and Châteauneuf up-river of that city. With the capture also of Olivet, a suburb of Orleans on the south bank of the river, the city was finally isolated. In order to make defence easier the French had destroyed large areas of its suburbs outside the walls: among them 'many excellent houses, including upward of twelve Churches belonging to four orders of Mendicant friars, with several fine houses of recreation for the burghers of Orleans. By thus doing they could discharge cannons freely all round.'[10] By November, 1428 Salisbury was on the point of launching an assault, and the morale of the defenders was so low that it would almost certainly have been successful. Instead, tragedy struck and this was the real turning-point in the war. It was by pure chance that Salisbury was killed at such a crucial moment.

The walled city of Orleans lies on the north bank of the River Loire, which then was some 400 yards wide at this point, shallow and rapid but navigable, with numerous sandbanks and islands. It was spanned by a bridge of nineteen arches. On the southernmost arch, and separated from the bank by a drawbridge, a fort with two towers called Les Tourelles had been built. This fort had been Salisbury's first objective, and had fallen remarkably easily considering its strength. The French had destroyed two of the arches of the bridge as they retreated across the river into the city, with its massive walls, towers and bastions, all of which housed numerous cannons. Some of these were exceedingly powerful, and one was seen to sink a barge moving on the river at a range of about 1,400 yards.[11]

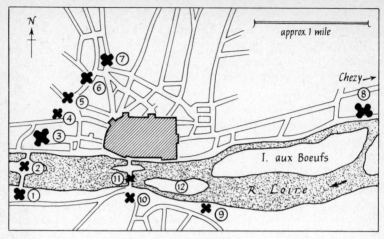

Orleans, 1428

Key
1. Bastille du Champ de St. Privé
2. Bastille d'Ile de Charlemagne
3. Bastille de St. Laurent (Talbot's HQ)
4. Bastille de la Croix Boissé
5. Bastille dez douze Pierres (nicknamed 'London')
6. Bastille de Pressoir Ars (nicknamed 'Rouen')
7. Bastille de St. Pouair (nicknamed 'Paris')
8. Bastille de St. Loup (Suffolk in command)
9. Bastille de St. Jean le Blanc
10. Bastille des Augustins
11. Les Tourelles
12. Ile de St. Aignan

As bad luck would have it, just at the moment that
Salisbury, Sir Thomas Gargrave and Sir William Glasdale
were in one of the Tourelles examining the French defences,
the small son of one of the French gunners was playing about
among the cannons. It was a quiet moment when the French
gunners had gone to their dinner (Salisbury had timed his visit
with this in view), and the lad, either for a lark or because he
spotted the English party in the Tourelles, touched off one of
the cannons. Salisbury heard the shot coming and ducked.
The cannon-ball hit the lintel of the window dislodging an
iron bar which struck Salisbury on the side of his face
removing half of it. They carried him to Meung, where he
died eight days later, on 3rd November, after suffering

terrible pain. Gargave too was mortally wounded, but Glasdale escaped.

The discipline of the English soldiers had been poor, and there was much desertion and robbery. Even the Church at Cléry had been plundered and, locally, Salisbury's calamitous death was regarded as Divine punishment for sacrilege. [12] Nevertheless there can be no doubt that, but for his death, Salisbury would have taken Orleans by assault in the very near future. As it was, he was succeeded by the timid and incompetent Suffolk, who tamely withdrew the army into Winter quarters in surrounding towns, leaving only an isolated garrison under Sir William Glasdale in the Tourelles. That was the position for three weeks and it speaks volumes for the low state of the French morale that, although they were in overwhelming strength and under the command of the able Dunois, the garrison made no move.

Bedford still resolutely refused to take command himself but, having no confidence in Suffolk, appointed John Talbot joint commander of the besieging force. It was an unenviable position for Talbot, but he took with him a redoubtable old friend, Lord Scales, and arrived at Orleans on December 1st, 1428.

He was soon able to persuade Suffolk that the army should move back at once into its siege positions as, now that the opportunity of an assault had been lost, they would have to revert to the normal siege process of isolation, mining and bombardment. But here there were some abnormal difficulties. The perimeter of the city was 2,000 yards. To construct a besieging line 700 yards outside the walls would require nearly 4,000 yards of fortifications, including any works on the south bank of the river. These would not only take weeks to construct but, when completed, there would not be enough soldiers to man them. This shortage was made more acute on 17th April when Philip of Burgundy, who had been in touch with Charles since Salisbury's death, ordered the Burgundian contingent of 1,500 men to withdraw from Orleans. [13]

Suffolk and Talbot decided to compromise. Talbot and Scales did not consider it likely that an attempt to relieve the city would be made from upstream of it. There were some empty barges moored under the walls but, apart from using them, the garrison had no way of crossing the river or coming at the Tourelles from upstream. In any case it would be easy to put a boom across the river up near St. Loup. They decided to establish a fort there and, with what they considered to be considerable tact, Talbot and Scales asked Suffolk to take command of that whole segment of the line. John Talbot set up his own headquarters at St. Laurent, some 800 yards downstream of the Tourelles, but on the north bank of the river (see Map, page 86). Between St. Laurent and the Tourelles there was a fort on the Ile de Charlemagne, and this seemed to make the whole river frontage reasonably secure from St. Loup down to St. Laurent. From St. Laurent round to the north-east Talbot constructed a line of forts connected by communication trenches. By April, 1429 four of these had been constructed, but even so there was still a gap of some 2,000 yards between the end fort and St. Loup. Moreover it was screened by woods, so that it was fairly easy for small bands with loads of provisions to run the gauntlet into the city.

As early as March, intelligence sources reported that the Dauphin was bestirring himself. He was said to be raising a relieving force at Blois, forty miles downstream of Orleans, under Charles of Bourbon, Count of Clermont. In March, too, a most curious document had appeared.[14] It was super-scribed to: "The Duke of Bedford, so-called Regent of the Kingdom of France, or to his lieutenants before the city of Orleans" but it is uncertain how or when it came into the hands of Bedford or Talbot. It is dated March 22nd, 1429:

"Jhesus Maria. King of England and you, Duke of Bedford calling yourself Regent of France: William de la Pole, Earl of Suffolk; John, Lord Talbot, and you, Thomas, Lord Scales, calling yourselves lieutenants of the said Bedford . . . deliver the keys of all the good towns you have taken and violated in France to the Maid (La Pucelle) who has been sent by God the King of Heaven . . . go away, for God's sake, back to your own country: otherwise await news of La Pucelle who will soon visit you to your great detriment. (Alès vous en, en vos pais, de par Dieu, et se ainssi ne le faictes, attendés les nouvelles de la Pucelle qui vous ira veoir briefment à vostre bien grant domaige.)"

The English dismissed the document as an outrageous piece of impertinence, and classed as empty rumour the story that a girl had gained the ear of the Dauphin, alleging that she was under Divine guidance. Lent was approaching, when the army would find it difficult to obtain a fish diet. Bedford fitted out a convoy in Paris under the command of Sir John Fastolf, consisting of 300 wagon-loads of salted herrings and other commodities. It was escorted by 1,000 mounted archers and some Paris Militiamen.[15] The convoy had reached the little village of Rouvray, five miles north of Janville, when it was intercepted by Count Clermont from Blois. With great ingenuity and presence of mind Fastolf, whose wagon-train stretched over three miles, formed them into a circle with just two openings. These openings he defended with archers, while the remainder of his little force, with their animals, took cover inside.

Clermont, perplexed by this hedgehog-like defence, brought up some small cannon and directed their fire at the wagons. Herrings flew in all directions but casualties were few. Then, luckily for Fastolf, a Scottish contingent disobeyed Clermont's orders and attacked. They suffered a bloody repulse by the archers. The French men-at-arms then charged. They too were driven off, leaving many men and horses impaled on the archers' staves. At this point Fastolf told his men to mount and they delivered a sharp counter-attack. The enemy turned and fled. The battle came to be known as the Battle of the Herrings. A few days later Fastolf triumphantly led his convoy into the English camp in front of Orleans.

The extent of the despondency of the French can be gauged by the fact that, about this time John Talbot received a deputation from the Garrison of Orleans who wished to start negotiations for surrender. But the real truth was that the men and money vital for the success of the siege were lacking. It was costing 40,000 Livres tournois a month and, in March, Bedford was compelled to sacrifice part of his own salary and to order all officials, whatever their rank, to "lend" a quarter of a year's salary to be used exclusively for the siege. Those who were not prepared to do so with good grace would forfeit six months' pay.[16] Yet though it seemed that Talbot had, after all, been able to retrieve the disaster of Salisbury's death, it was not to be. A few weeks later the Dauphin's army moved out of Blois under the command of the Duke d'Alençon, but with the girl, Jeanne d'Arc, in the van. She was dramatically clad in a full suit of plate armour and accompanied by a large body of priests. Psalms and hymns were sung on the march instead of the usual bawdy songs common to all armies on the move; swearing was prohibited and daily Mass was compulsory for everyone. After so many years of superiority in morale and fighting ability, John Talbot and his fellow commanders found it difficult to take this charade seriously. It was thus to their considerable surprise that they saw the Dauphinist army move on upstream of Orleans on the south bank, as if to gain access to the city by capturing the Tourelles. The system of defences there was such that Talbot was confident that they would not be captured.

Nevertheless the French army, with its considerable convoy of supplies, continued on upstream and, from his position at St. Laurent, Talbot was surprised to hear the sound of an attack developing on the Augustins' fortifications, and later of a further attack on Suffolk's position at St. Loup. In fact, as he learned later, those attacks were demonstrations to divert attention. The wind, which had been blowing steadily from the east, swung round to the west and Dunois was able to sail those empty barges upstream as far as Chézy. That he was able to do so, and that they were then able to return downstream laden with supplies, was due to Suffolk's negligence. He and Talbot had agreed that he should place a boom across the river at St. Loup, and he had failed to do so. Dunois had learned of this and had passed the information on to Alençon. It was a costly, indeed a fatal, mistake.

CHATER VIII

ON MAY 3rd, 1429, the relieving army entered Orleans, led by Jeanne d'Arc, who claimed that Divine help was responsible for the change of direction of the wind and hence for the relief of the city. It may have been so, but Suffolk's stupidity contributed. Until then nobody had attached much importance to the presence of the girl. Later that same day, while another diversionary attack was being made on Fort St. Loup, she galloped out of the town and joined the attackers, inspiring them with such enthusiasm that they captured the position. [1]

The ferocity with which this attack was pressed home and sustained took Talbot by surprise, and he left his headquarters at St. Laurent and moved round the north-east perimeter picking up men as he passed each fort with the intention of relieving St. Loup. Dunois, however, saw his intention from his position on the City walls and sent out a covering force to intercept him. The two forces met at Fort Paris, and a sharp little engagement took place before Talbot, seeing smoke rising from the burning fort at St. Loup, realised he was too late to relieve it and withdrew his men inside his own lines.

The next day was Ascension Day and Jeanne d'Arc refused to make any military move. She had sent an earlier demand by Herald to Talbot that he should give up the siege. She now addressed a further letter [2] to the besieging army:

"You, men of England, who have no right to be in this kingdom of France, the King of Heaven commands you through me, Jeanne la Pucelle, to abandon your forts and to go back where you belong: which if you fail to do, I will make such a ha-hai as will be eternally remembered. I am writing to you for the third and last time. I shall not write any more. Jhesus Maria. Jehanne la Pucelle."

She added a postscript: "I would have sent you my letter in a more honourable manner but you detain my Herald called Guienne. Please send him back to me and I will send back some of your people captured at Saint Loup for they are not all dead."

She then fastened the letter to an arrow and ordered a

cross-bowman to shoot it into the English camp, shouting "Read, here is news." The English evidently did not take it very seriously for they replied with derisive shouts of "Ah, news from the harlot of the Armagnacs". Thereupon, it is said, Jeanne appealed to God and burst into floods of tears.

On May 6th, Dunois launched an attack on the Tourelles. His striking force crossed by boat to the Isle of St. Antoine, whence they could now reach the south bank and join the attack being made by Clermont's men. John Talbot was cut off from the Tourelles, which no reinforcements could now reach. It has since been calculated that some 4,000 French were concentrated against the 500 English in the Augustins' Fort and the Tourelles, yet the struggle went on all day and by the evening only the former had been captured.

Even now the English Commanders could hardly believe the unaccustomed fury of the French attack. Gradually it dawned upon them that Jeanne d'Arc was its inspiration, that the French morale, their will to win, which had been so conspicuously lacking for many years, had been replaced by an almost fanatical fervour.

The next morning, May 7th, the attack on the Tourelles was resumed. With a new strategy, guns and scaling ladders were brought into action: even a fire-ship was rigged up and floated downstream beneath the drawbridge which led from the earthworks into the Tourelles. The drawbridge caught fire and, as the little garrison withdrew across it, it collapsed. The last man to attempt the crossing was the gallant Glasdale, who had so recently escaped death with Salisbury. He was cast into the river and drowned.

But still the men in the Tourelles fought on. At last the powder for their cannons began to fail, until the charges were so small that the shots merely rolled out of the muzzles and fell harmlessly into the water. The end came when those inside the City managed, with great ingenuity, to bridge the damaged arches of the bridge so that the Tourelles could be attacked from both sides.* The small remnant of the garrison was then forced, at long last, to surrender. Some hours later the

---

*Some echoes of this are to be found in the account books of the City of Orleans for 1429:

"Paid 40 sous for a heavy piece of wood obtained from Jean Bazin when the Tourelles were won from the English to put across the

The Count of Dunois, a statue at the castle of Châteaudun
(Photo. Archives Photographiques, Paris)

besiegers heard cheering as Jeanne d'Arc rode her grey charger across the bridge into Orleans.

The English had never had numerical superiority at Orleans, and now their superior morale had disappeared overnight. The town walls were still intact, so that an assault and a continuation of the siege were both out of the question. Yet John Talbot was still reluctant to admit defeat. On the morning of May 8th he moved his men out of their siege lines in full battle array, and advanced into the open space before the walls. There he drew them up and waited, silently challenging Dunois and his men to come out and fight. For two long hours they waited, but from the city came no indication of a desire for battle. At last Talbot gave the order and the whole army marched silently away to the north.

The only incident which attended their departure from Orleans concerned Talbot's Chaplain, an Augustin Friar named Anselm. During the siege he had taken upon himself to care for one of the prisoners, the Bastard du Barr, who was awaiting ransom and who was held in fetters. Father Anselm used to see that he was regularly fed. When the army marched away, Father Anselm, loath no doubt to see a ransom lost, partially freed du Barr's feet and led him away too. Apparently du Barr seized his opportunity, turned the tables on Father Anselm and, to add insult to injury, made him carry him, still in his fetters, back to Orleans. (4)

Talbot was bitterly angry with Suffolk for his fatal omission to place a boom across the Loire, and after the relief of Orleans the two commanders were hardly on speaking terms. Nevertheless they conferred as to what they should do next and the decision at which they arrived has since been criticised as a failure to keep their army concentrated at one point. Such critics forget that the English still believed that discrepancy in numbers between themselves and the French mattered little: so, rightly or wrongly, they decided that Suffolk should go east to Jargeau, and that Scales and Talbot should occupy Meung and Beaugency. From those positions they could harry Dunois' lines of communication, and pose the greatest threat to Orleans until Bedford could relieve the position.

---

broken arches of the bridge.

"Given to Champeaux and other carpenters 16 sous to go and drink on the day the Tourelles were won."(3)

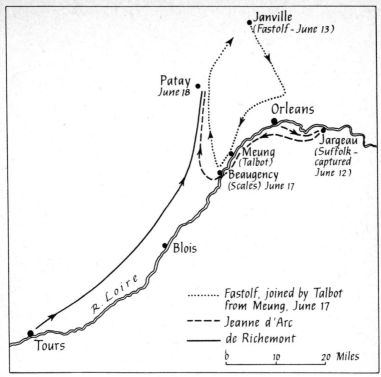

Patay Campaign

Meanwhile Jeanne d'Arc had succeeded in persuading the Dauphin to raise a larger army, and she was unwittingly helped by a move which Fastolf made towards Blois. His was a name rather like John Talbot's, of which the French were in awe, and his threatened attack added strength to Jeanne's arguments. It was thus that, early in June, Alençon, with Jeanne in company, joined forces with Dunois' Orleans contingent to form a well-equipped army of some 8,000 men. Yet, as Alençon testified later, even with such superiority of strength, there was much hesitation and debate before an attack was launched against Jargeau. This was only resolved by the scoldings of Jeanne who urged an immediate assault. [5] There was a skirmish outside the walls in which she again distinguished herself by her courage. That evening she approached the walls completely alone and uttered the astonishing challenge to Suffolk to "surrender the town to the

King of Heaven and to King Charles and depart or it will be the worse for you". [6]

Suffolk did, in fact, send a herald to negotiate with Dunois, but nothing came of it and, next day, the bombardment of the walls began. This was so successful that the French were able to mount an assault on them within a matter of days, and Jeanne herself took a prominent part. The town fell and Suffolk surrendered himself to a squire named Guillaume Regnault after first knighting him, so that, according to the traditions of chivalry, it might be said that he had been captured by a knight. [7]

Every man of the garrison was put to the sword, and the Church was looted. It seemed that there were limits to the authority which Jeanne could wield. Jargeau fell on June 12th, the Sunday of a memorable week of success for the French.

But more was to follow. Alençon and Dunois acted with surprising energy. On Monday they moved back to Orleans, and on Wednesday continued on along the south bank of the river towards Meung and Beaugency. They reached the bridge at Meung at nightfall and over-ran a small defensive position at its southern end. But, on Thursday, instead of crossing the bridge to attack Meung, they continued along the river to Beaugency. There, on Friday, the siege artillery which had been so successfully employed at Jargeau opened up on the little town. Matthew Gough, who had played such a notable part in John Talbot's recapture of Le Mans, and who had since been knighted, was in command. Hopelessly outnumbered and despairing of relief, he compounded with Alençon to quit the town, his troops taking their arms with them. He was unaware that Fastolf's relieving army was halted only two miles away.

Fastolf had set out on June 5th to relieve or reinforce Jargeau. He may have managed to collect some 3,000 men, but probably not as many. All the best and most active soldiers from the Normandy garrisons had already been taken and the quality of his army was very poor: it included a considerable number of "faux Français", mercenaries who had taken service under the Anglo-Burgundian banner and who were generally known to be unreliable. Sir John Fastolf was well aware of this and it may explain much of what was to follow. It has to be noted however that Waurin, who may have been a little biased, and who was now serving under Fastolf, considered the men "well chosen". [8]

When Fastolf reached Janville he realised that he was too late to relieve Jargeau and so, on June 16th, when he had joined forces with Talbot, they moved together towards Beaugency. Talbot had with him his personal headquarter force, gallant men and experienced soldiers, but a mere handful: 40 lances and 200 mounted archers. (A "lance" was a self-contained mounted unit consisting of a man-at-arms, a swordsman, two archers, one valet-aux-armes, and a page.)

Waurin, who was present, relates that on Thursday, Talbot and Fastolf and Rempston had déjeuner together [9] and debated what they should do. Talbot was still confident of his superior fighting power; Fastolf was not. He urged that they should fall back in a defensive action. John Talbot violently opposed such a defeatist attitude, and went so far as to say that, even if Fastolf would not come with him, he would go to the relief of Gough in Beaugency. This forced Fastolf's hand and reluctantly he agreed to move forward, although he continued up to the last moment to try to dissuade Talbot from what he considered a very rash move. [10]

They arrived at Meung and found the south end of the bridge held by the French. About two miles short of Beaugency the road mounts a slight ridge and from there they could see a second ridge about 800 yards away on which the French army was being drawn up in battle array. They halted, deployed their men, and waited. Nothing happened. At last they sent a Herald forward with the proposal that three knights from each army should fight out the issue between them. The French ignored the challenge. Fastolf and Talbot decided that they must fall back on Meung, cross the bridge there and approach Beaugency along the south bank, taking the French position from the flank.

In preparation for the attack next day Talbot arranged for his cannons to bombard Meung bridge during the night. So far as is known this had never been done before and when, at dawn, the assault went in, it made good progress. But then Sir Matthew Gough himself appeared to tell Talbot that Beaugency had fallen. This settled the matter, but it also placed the English army in a highly dangerous position. Talbot realised that he must retreat to Janville with all speed.

His position was in reality even more dangerous than he knew. To Alençon's considerable chagrin, Arthur de Richemont had marched into his camp with 1,000 Breton soldiers. He had, in actual fact, been driven from the Dauphin's Court in disgrace and Charles had forbidden Alençon to receive him. Jeanne d'Arc, however, insisted on greeting him enthusiastically[11] though accounts vary according to the loyalty of the narrator. The narrative which follows is largely taken from the *Chronicles* of Waurin, who was present, and from Monstrelet who may or may not have copied Waurin.[12]

It was now Saturday, a bare six days since Jeanne had entered Jargeau. John Talbot was making what speed he could towards Janville. Patay, eighteen miles to the north, seemed to offer a defensive position of a sort. There the hedged road from Lignarolles to Coinces crosses the old Roman road near the bottom of a shallow dip in the ground. A few hundred yards further on there is a ridge. The plan was for Fastolf to hold the ridge while Talbot's archers occupied forward positions in the scrub and along the line of the hedge. Fastolf did not like the position but Talbot considered that it was the best available. Scales, Rempston and Hungerford, all men of experience, agreed with him.

They set about deploying in their positions and hammering in their stakes. Danger was more imminent than they thought, for the French advanced-guard composed of specially selected men, all well mounted, under the command of La Hire and Poton de Xantrailles, were only four miles away. The main body, led by Alençon and Dunois, were further back, and Jeanne d'Arc and de Richemont were with the rearguard. An army of some 6,000 men in all was advancing on fewer than 3,000.

It was about two o'clock in the afternoon when suddenly a stag ran down the line of archers and was naturally pursued by raucous shouts and "halloo's". That, as it turned out, was the first intimation Xantrailles' scouts had of the English position.

Talbot was near his command post, which consisted of a prominent bush not far from the cross-roads. He was on foot, supervising the deployment of the archers, when he heard a shout and, looking up, saw the leading ranks of Frenchmen lining the top of the rise. His herald had seen them a moment earlier and ran towards him with his horse. The archers dropped whatever they were doing and fired indiscriminately at the charging Frenchmen. Talbot had one foot in the stirrup when a stunning blow hit him in the back.

CHAPTER IX

THE FRENCH VICTORY at Patay was complete and the English casualties were very heavy. They had, for the first time, been roundly defeated in battle. Not only had the great John Talbot been taken prisoner, but nearly all the junior commanders had also: Scales, Rempston and Hungerford. A window in Patay Church depicts the incident. Only Fastolf had escaped with some 60 of his men, amongst whom was Waurin. [1] He had managed to elude Alençon's pursuit, but when he reached Paris he was accused of cowardice and of leaving John Talbot to his death. Bedford even went so far as to deprive him of the Order of the Garter, which he had only recently been awarded. It was the most severe penalty that chivalry could exact. Talbot himself was taken to a house in the village of Patay, in a road which is still called La Rue Talbot. His wound was so severe that he received Holy Unction and, feeling certain that he was going to die, he asked that his body should be buried in the Porch of Whitchurch Church "that, as members of my guard have stood over and defended me while living, they and their children for ever should walk over me when dead".

The victory at Patay and the capture of Talbot raised French morale to its peak. It was less than a week since Jeanne d'Arc had marched out of Orleans, but it had been a week of dazzling success. It was, in fact, the only campaign conducted entirely under her inspiration, and it places her among the front rank of intuitive commanders. Her eyes were now set on the Coronation of the Dauphin at Rheims. Thither, with considerable difficulty, she was able to drag him and he was crowned Charles VII on July 16th, 1429. Jeanne's mission was accomplished and it would have been well for France, for England and for Jeanne herself if she had then retired to her native Domremy.

John Talbot did not die but made a slow recovery. As soon as he was well enough to be moved he was taken to Bourges and paroled. All the other commanders had ransomed themselves immediately, but Talbot's ransom figure was so high that it was a matter for negotiation between France and

100

England. These started as soon as it was known that he would not die, but they dragged on during the months that followed. His capture had caused great despondency in London, where a ransom fund was started. Events, however, made it unnecessary.

As soon as John Talbot heard of Fastolf's disgrace he sent word to Bedford exonerating Fastolf. The Garter was restored to Fastolf and he was given another command. Hall comments, however, that this was done "against the mind of Lord Talbot".[2]

John Talbot was held prisoner from June 1429 until November 1431 and it was thus that he saw the final tragic stages of Jeanne's meteoric career from the French head-quarters at Bourges. He saw her persuade the reluctant King Charles to campaign towards Paris. He, poor man, kept finding reasons for turning southwards, but she bullied and cajoled him until they succeeded in reaching the village of Montmartre. There she insisted that the attack on Paris itself should be pressed home. Yet when it was, and, in the face of fierce Burgundian resistance, Jeanne fell wounded, Charles withdrew to Senlis with, apparently, no consideration for the safety of the girl to whom he owed so much.

In the Autumn of 1429 the tide once more turned against the French. Burgundy and Bedford reconciled their differences and Bedford managed to re-assert his control over Normandy. He was even able to return to England for the Coronation of the boy King Henry VI at Westminster, on November 6th.

By December 1430, there appears to have been good enough reason to believe that the Talbot ransom negotiations might be successfully concluded for cash to be sent over to France. On January 8th, Warwick together with the Archbishops of York and Canterbury, Gloucester, Beaufort and Barthou (on behalf of Burgundy), showed a most unusual degree of unanimity in addressing a note to the King which read as follows:[3]

"May it please the King, our most sovereign Lord, to grant to your humble liegeman, John Lord Talbot, licence (he being in your ward in France and at this time put upon his redemption and ransom) to have out of your realm the sum of 8,000 marks* or less, of your coin of the same your realm, and also that his people and servants may convey and carry it to the said Lord for the cause aforesaid without hindrance of your heirs. For the sake of God and as an act of charity, the Statute thereupon made to the contrary not withstanding".

signed   H. Gloucester   H. Cardinal
                H. Cantuar   J. Ebor
                J. Barthou   R. Warwick

The King agreed this two days later, but the negotiations broke down.

During the same month Bedford resumed the offensive, and in April a new army landed at Calais under Cardinal Beaufort. There he was joined by the King, then aged eight. Philip of Burgundy also assembled an army, at Mondidier, 30 miles north west of Compiègne. Jeanne, hearing of these moves, took a mere handful of men to Compiègne which she entered on May 13th. Duke Philip was nominally besieging the town but the French could, in fact, come and go comparatively freely. Included in Duke Philip's army was an English detachment under Sir John Montgomery. During the next few days Jeanne took part in some rather insignificant manoeuvres but, on May 24th, she made a more serious sortie with about 500 men. Crossing a long causeway, her men surprised and scattered a Burgundian outpost. But it so happened that Duke John of Luxemburg was reconnoitring a hill nearby just at that moment. He sent men to intercept Jeanne and a fierce fight ensued in which she showed outstanding courage. Matters seemed to be going well for her when suddenly Montgomery's men attacked her party in the rear. Most of them fled, Jeanne herself was driven off the causeway, which cut off her retreat. She was then driven by Montgomery into the arms of the Burgundians, and captured by them.

Her trial by the Burgundian Church hierarchy and her execution on May 30th, 1431 by the English army, as the effective civil power of the land, is not part of John Talbot's story. He experienced at first hand the grief and anger which filled the hearts of the French and it may be that it was his sympathetic reaction to this event which so endeared him to his French opponents in later years. Miss Sackville-West suggests[4] that Charles was remiss in his duty to Jeanne d'Arc

---

*Equivalent to approximately £5,000 (see previous page)

in failing to attempt to exchange her for John Talbot, although she admits that the English would have been unlikely to agree to such a suggestion.

Meanwhile it was June 1431 that, by a great stroke of luck, Warwick, when attacking a French force near Savignies captured a party of 60 men led by no less a person than Poton de Xantrailles. Negotiations were started immediately[5] for his exchange with John Talbot, and these were brought to a successful conclusion in November.[6]

By that time John Talbot had lost touch with affairs in England. In April 1431 there had been serious riots in the Midlands. A man called Jack Sharpe had roused popular resentment against the wealth and profligacy of the Bishops, Abbots and Priors, advocating that the Crown should take over their possessions. Gloucester had acted swiftly and firmly to suppress what appeared to be a resurgence of Lollardism. He had also attempted to curtail Beaufort's power by depriving him of his See on the grounds, admitted as correct by the Bishop of Worcester, that Beaufort had procured from Rome an exemption of himself and his See from the juris-diction of Canterbury: a serious threat to the established authority. The attempt failed, but it was only one of many moves and counter-moves in the quarrel between Gloucester and Beaufort. Their rivalries and struggles for power went on, becoming more and more bitter as the years passed. They form a dark background to the latter years of John Talbot's life, though he himself kept aloof from them. He was the more respected on that account. But, so long as he was Regent, Bedford was always master of the situation and no serious harm was done to the national interest. Moreover Gloucester became more and more immersed in literature and the arts, and so was less inclined to engage in conflict with Beaufort. Nevertheless the struggle was serious enough and the tension high enough for the issue of Parliamentary Writs enjoining Norfolk, Suffolk, Huntingdon, Stafford, Northumberland, Salisbury and Cromwell not to bring with them to Parliament more than their usual essential retainers.

The year 1432 saw some set-backs to England. Chartres fell to the French in March. Bedford made the siege of Lagny his main summer objective; but the French put up a spirited defence, the weather became unbearably hot and Bedford himself suffered a heat-stroke, probably from over exertion. He never fully recovered from this and, when Dunois brought up a relieving army, he regretfully abandoned the siege. Soon afterwards his beloved wife, Anne, died in Paris. She had been lying ill there for many months.

Coming on the top of his own illness, Anne's death was a heavy blow for Bedford; it was also a political disaster. It weakened still further the precarious Burgundian alliance. Bedford faced these troubles with great courage and, in 1433 he married Jaquetta St. Pol, niece of Burgundy's chief Captain, in the hope that this would strengthen the alliance. Sadly it had the opposite effect. Burgundy took offence[7] because Jaquetta, as wife of the Regent, was given precedence over the Duchess, his wife. Bedford's troubles were not confined to France. People in England began to attribute the deteriorating position there to incompetence, even treachery, on his part.

Bedford returned to England in the summer of 1433 to face his enemies in Parliament, when it met in July, and his dominating presence had the usual calming effect. In October Parliament had to be prorogued because of fear of the plague, which was raging more fiercely than ever that year. But tension was still so high that it met in special session on November 24th to petition the King to keep Bedford in England to prevent civil war. Bedford agreed, although he insisted on being given full power to dominate the Council of State. An uneasy winter followed, in the course of which the two brothers, Bedford and Gloucester had a violent and bitter quarrel.

In the spring of 1434 the peasants of Normandy staged a major uprising, directed mainly against the depredations of the ill-disciplined English garrisons. Arundel was already in France and advancing on Chartres, but Bedford felt that his own presence was now more necessary in France than in England. He was accompanied by John Talbot, who had been in England since his release. Hall writes:[8] "The presence of this renowned captain (a marvellous thing it is to say) so encouraged the hearts of the English nation that they thought nothing able to resist their puysance and so discouraged the hearts of the Frenchmen that they were in doubt which it was better, to fight or to fly. And this was not without cause for surely he was a chosen captain and, in martial feats, a man fully instructed and his courage and practice in war was fearful to the French nation . . ."

Talbot took with him 800 picked men, and went first to Rouen. From there he attacked and captured Gisors, and then went on to confer with Bedford in Paris. They agreed that a strong, swift, punitive campaign was required and that, as Arundel was working south west of Paris, Talbot should do a sweep north east. Lisle Adam with 800 Burgundians would accompany him. News of his approach always preceded him and, as often as not, castle garrisons and towns came out to surrender to him. He found Gony Castle abandoned, destroyed it and moved on. A short siege of Creil followed. Beaumont, Pont de St. Lawrence, whose Captain was a nephew of Xantrailles, Neuf-Ville, La Rouge Maison, Crespy (which had to be taken by assault) and finally Clermont; all these towns fell and when John Talbot entered Paris he did so with many valuable prisoners and much booty.

The Exchequer enumeration of English garrisons in France in 1421 shows that there were then 30, held by 2,436 men. In 1434, 26 garrisons were held by 970 men. [9] The comparison gives some idea of the problem which now faced Talbot in trying to hold Normandy for England. It also shows how starved he and Bedford were for funds, for if there had been more money there would have been more soldiers. This in turn meant that their work as Commanders was hard and incessant. What was lacking in numbers had to be made up by increased mobility.

In addition to the military aspect of their work, they had to administer the country, or at least to oversee its administration. This involved the appointment of local officials, who were generally Normans loyal to the English. They collected and paid into the Exchequer local taxes such as the Salt Tax. In an effort to improve the efficiency of garrisons John Talbot compiled very detailed regulations for them. These covered general discipline, behaviour towards the populace, treatment of prisoners, payment for food and for fodder, cleanliness etc. They even dictated penalties for spreading sickness. Talbot also laid down that, when out on active service, every seven men should provide a scaling ladder and every two yeomen a pavise or large wooden shield. Every archer had to provide his

own oak stake. These and many other details of civil and
military administration issued under Talbot's direction show
that, in addition to being an enterprising commander he had
a keen eye for detail.

A revolt by the peasants of Normandy occurred in 1434, but
it was quickly suppressed and all seemed to be going well when
suddenly the scene changed. Philip of Burgundy announced
that he was ready to make his peace with King Charles, and
invited Bedford to join him in the negotiations. Bedford had
always feared some such move, and angrily refused. His
military operations were making much headway, and indeed
he felt that at long last they might be bringing the war to a
successful conclusion. This was no moment at which to talk of
peace negotiations. He had the full support of Scales,
Warwick, Talbot and, until his death during the summer,
Arundel.

But Burgundy was now intent on peace, and he arranged to
meet the Duke of Bourbon at Nevers. They agreed that a
peace conference should take place at Arras in 1435. Meeting
nothing but opposition from Bedford, they sent envoys over his
head direct to King Henry in England. That young man had
always disliked the war in France and, in addition, he was
prone to listen mainly to the advice of Cardinal Beaufort and
his friends. These were strongly in favour of bringing an end to
the war. Thus it was that the King agreed that an English
deputation should attend the proposed Conference in a
watching capacity. It arrived at Arras in the first week of July
and consisted of the Archbishop of York, Lords Suffolk and
Hungerford, and Raoul le Sage, an official from the staff of
the Archbishop of Canterbury. [10] All were friends of
Beaufort's. A day or two later the French delegation arrived:
there were 400 of them. Burgundy, who had arrived with his
delegates a few days earlier, hurried round making sure that
both the English and the French delegates felt that they were
equally welcome. [11] In order to ensure that no "accident"
happened in the conference area, Burgundy ordered that 300
commissaries should patrol the town night and day. [12]
Nevertheless, Burgundy's efforts were nearly wrecked when it
was heard that La Hire and Xantrailles were raiding into
Burgundy only thirty miles away. However, members of all
three delegations took to their horses and the discomforted

raiders retired.

Eventually the conference was opened, with great pomp and ceremony. Apart from the main delegations, the whole of Europe seemed to be represented. There were representatives of the Kings of Seville, Arragon, Navarre, Portugal. Denmark, Venice, Florence, and the Pope of Rome. [13] The proceedings took place in the Abbey St. Waast.

Elsewhere the war continued unabated. Scales, Warwick and Talbot were in the field and, to their great pleasure, they were joined for a time by the Burgundian Lisle Adam. It was to be the last occasion on which English and Burgundian soldiers fought side by side. Within a few weeks they were on opposite sides in the war, and, to quote Monstrelet, [14] "thus was a total change made in the public affairs of France and England and just contrary to what had been before".

Meanwhile the Conference was making some progress, at least between the two main parties. The English delegation, in spite of its inclination to peace, deeply mistrusted the close confabulation which went on between Burgundy and France. By the end of August it was clear that they were united in wanting to persuade Henry VI to renounce his title to the French Crown. Even Beaufort would not concede that point, for he knew that the people of England would never forgive him if he did. On September 6th he withdrew his delegation, and Burgundy and France made peace with one another.

During all these months Bedford, who was still unwell from the campaign of the previous year, had waited anxiously in Rouen. He had joined John Talbot in front of St. Denys for some weeks, but he was sick at heart and everyone could see it. He had lost his beloved wife only a year or so previously, he was ill and tired, and now the insipid Henry, under the thumb of Cardinal Beaufort, was destroying all that he, Bedford and Henry V before him had fought so hard to achieve. They were throwing away what the English regarded as their rightful heritage, and there was nothing that Bedford could do to prevent it. He died on September 14th, and John Talbot mourned the loss of a man who had been his counsellor, his comrade-in-arms and his friend for nearly half a century: the consequences both for England and for Talbot could not be other than calamitous.

CHAPTER X

JOHN TALBOT was now supreme commander in France. But the peace party led by Beaufort, with growing influence on the part of Suffolk, was gaining strength in England. Talbot could expect little support from them. Without Bedford's restraining influence they would forge ahead, and Gloucester, already a weakening influence, would soon be eclipsed. The Duke of York, an energetic, able young man aged 24, was now the mainstay of those who wanted England to retain her French possessions, and he was appointed "Regent of France". [1]

But there was another group of people for whom both John and his wife had much sympathy. Over the decades of war, scores of English yeomen had settled in French towns, villages and farms. In Normandy, Maine and Anjou, as also in Gascony, there were areas where a transfer of allegiance to King Charles of France would be regarded as treason. The handing over of such territories would create a refugee problem. It was true that some of the English had been in France for so long, and had intermarried with the French so much, that they had no great incentive to fight for one side or the other: that meant that, in some towns, men with English names had become so French that it was difficult to know who could or could not be trusted. Such was the involved position which, at the age of about fifty-one, now confronted Talbot.

In 1435 the Duke of York arrived in France, to work in double harness with Talbot. Feeling between the Burgundians and the English was now extremely bad, and indeed a state of war had been declared between them. [2] Burgundy persuaded the Flemings to attack Calais, while he himself attempted to blockade it by sea. However, this ploy proved to be something of a disaster, which was completed when Gloucester crossed the Channel and routed the Flemings.

York, obedient to his instructions, made an attempt to negotiate with King Charles, but nothing came of it and he and Talbot proceeded to carry on the war with renewed vigour. They had everything to gain and little to lose.

In January 1436 La Hire and Xantrailles penetrated right

up to the gates of Rouen, Talbot's headquarters. They had been told by French sympathisers that they would be admitted.[3] However, earlier that month, Talbot had appointed four English soldiers as roving scouts in the country-side around Rouen (at the high pay of 3s.4d. per day) to give "better warning of ambuscades and approaches of the enemy" and they foiled the plot.[4] The French fell back ten miles east, to the village of Ry, to await reinforcements. Talbot's scouts brought him news of this and, hurriedly collecting Scales and Kyriell, with 400 men, he galloped out of the city. Ry lies in a hollow surrounded on all sides by woods. Half a mile to the west of the village there is a ridge and there La Hire had placed his outposts. But he had not noticed that they were screened from his view. Silently Talbot's men over-powered them and then swept into Ry. Panic overtook the French, most of whom were in their billets. La Hire did his best to rally them but in vain. He was himself severely wounded but escaped on one of his men's horses.[5]

Meanwhile the Parisians rose against the English garrison there and, with the help of Lisle Adam, forced it to surrender. The Banner of Burgundy now flew over the city in place of the flag of St. George.

York then returned to England, convinced that his presence was necessary there to counteract that of the peace party. Gloucester's influence was comparatively insignificant: he was spending most of his time on his collection of rare books, some of which he now began to give to Oxford University.

Soon after York left France news reached Talbot that twelve burgesses of Gisors, the whole of the Town Council as it turned out, had sold it for cash to Xantrailles.[6] Talbot collected a force of 1,800 men and, taking Scales with him, made one of his rapid marches. They arrived entirely unexpectedly, recap-tured the town without difficulty, and hanged the treacherous burgesses over their own town gates.

Winter came early that year and was long and very hard.[7] John Talbot determined that Pontoise, some 20 miles north of Paris, should be his main objective. There was a certain grim irony about this choice, as it was garrisoned by Burgundians under the command of John's old friend and companion, Lisle Adam.

The town, as its name implies, was centered on a bridge

over the River Oise, which at this point was about 100 yards wide. It stood, too, on the direct road from Rouen to Paris, so it was of considerable strategical importance: it had indeed been described as the gateway to Paris from the north. The Castle towered above, and completely dominated the bridge, and the town's walls were strong and well designed. It was a most formidable obstacle, well stocked with stores and adequately garrisoned.

To attack this objective John Talbot took a picked force of 400 men and, to their great mystification, made each man carry a white sheet.[8] In the bitter cold of the night of 12th February, 1437, he made a forced march from Rouen, a distance of just over 50 miles. They reached the vicinity of Pontoise before anyone realised that an English force was on the move, still less in that particular area. As he had expected, the river was frozen so hard that they were able to cross it upstream of the bridge. Once on the other side he made a party of about a dozen men disguise themselves as villagers carrying hampers and baskets of food as if on their way to market. He guessed correctly that, as they would be approaching from the direction of Paris they would arouse no suspicion.

Next he detailed a scaling party, and these men wrapped themselves in the white sheets. The timing of the approach of these two parties had to be carefully arranged to take place early in the morning. All was quiet and peaceful and Lisle Adam was sound asleep in bed when suddenly a great shout rang out inside the town. "The Town is ours. St. George! Talbot!" This was the pre-arranged signal to be made by the market party.[9] The scaling party, their ladders already in position, then entered the town and opened the gates to John Talbot and the rest of his troops. Lisle Adam managed to escape with a few of his men, but they left behind them all their belongings and a great quantity of stores. The English hardly lost a man.

This was not quite the end of the affair. A large part of the object of the operation had been to raise English morale, and Talbot determined to raise it still further by pressing his attack home as far as Paris itself. It was a highly dangerous thing to do, but he and his men penetrated up to the very walls of Paris, crossed the moat, and actually placed their scaling

ladders in position. There they met intense fire from crossbows
and were forced to withdraw. John Talbot had never intended
to put his puny force into a major attack, but they knew that
they had severely shaken the French and the Burgundians,
and their spirits were high as they retired.

Some minor successes followed and York, who had again
returned to France, recovered Dieppe. Six months later
Talbot took the field again. The English still held two key
positions on each side of the Somme estuary: St. Valery and Le
Crotoy. The Burgundians were besieging the latter and had
appealed to the Duke of Luxemburg for reinforcements. He
stoutly refused to cross swords with his late allies, and Duke
Philip had to conduct the operation himself.

Le Crotoy was the nearest coastal town to Calais still in
English hands, and John Talbot sent representatives to
England urging that it should not be allowed to fall. Warwick,
his father-in-law, had reluctantly emerged from semi-
retirement to take over from York, and he enabled John to
take an army of about 5,000 men to relieve Le Crotoy. Talbot
made no attempt to conceal his approach or to achieve
surprise. Indeed he issued a challenge to Burgundy to fight in
the open. Duke Philip did not respond. Instead, he went in
person to Abbeville to strengthen the defences there.

As Abbeville appeared to be firmly held Talbot resolved to
emulate Edward III, and to cross the Somme by the famous
ford of Blanche Taque. As on that previous occasion, the tide
was partly up and the far shore was lined by Burgundian
archers with some cannons in support. They considered they
were in an impregnable position, and were completely taken
aback when, without even pausing, Talbot's men plunged
straight into the water and advanced towards them.[10] They
were dispersed with few English casualties. Talbot must have
had evidence of the poor quality of his opponents before
attempting such a hazardous operation, which serves to
emphasize the continuing superiority of the English professional soldiers over the French and Burgundian levies.

On reaching the far bank Talbot tried to entice the enemy
out into the open by ravaging the surrounding country. He
penetrated almost to Hesdin, Duke Philip's northern capital,
25 miles to the east, but to no effect. The reputation of the
'English Achilles' and his men was such that practically no

resistance was offered, wherever they went or whatever they did.

At length John Talbot turned towards Le Crotoy and, as he approached, the besiegers fled, leaving behind all their artillery and an immense quantity of stores. The garrison of Le Crotoy pursued them "shouting rudely at them as they would have done at a riotous mob". [11]

The English army returned to Rouen heavily laden with booty and in high spirits. Colonel Burne's comment on this campaign is that "Talbot had shown his versatility. His was no one-track mind: his methods had been entirely different from those employed heretofore: he had sized up his opponents correctly; one of the marks of military genius — and had achieved his aim with a minimum of bloodshed". [12]

It was indeed the fact that the English recovery since the death of Bedford, when all seemed lost, was almost entirely due to the energy and enterprise of Talbot; the ordinary folk in England were later to acknowledge this in their warm welcome on his return to England in 1442.

When events were moving so well in France, it was doubly disappointing for those engaged in the operations there to hear that the Council of State in England had decided, once more, to explore the possibilities of a peace settlement. Cardinal Beaufort had evolved the idea of sending to France the Duke of Orleans, captured at Agincourt, who had now been a prisoner in England for twenty four years. He would act as an intermediary, but would only be given his freedom if negotiations were successful. In the event they broke down once more over the question of King Henry's title to the Crown of France, and Orleans returned to his captivity in Stourton Castle, Wiltshire. His long imprisonment and his failure to obtain his ransom was primarily due to the feud between his family and that of Burgundy, following the murder of Duke John of Burgundy in 1419. Duke Philip would not agree to Orleans being released. [13]

During 1438 famine and plague devastated both England and France, and hostilities almost came to a halt except in Gascony. There, the English rule rested, not on the spears and bows of an alien garrison, but on the will and wish of the whole population. It had done so for three hundred years. King Charles tried to change this, but the English Council, moved by the Gascons' appeal for help, sent Huntingdon, much as they were later to send John Talbot, to drive the French invaders back. He did so without much difficulty.

Beaufort entered into tentative peace negotiations again in 1439, and this time a Conference was arranged. Both sides made it clear that they feared some treacherous act but eventually the conference took place on July 6th, at Calais. [14] Once more the negotiations were wrecked on the matter of sovereignty, but it was arranged that there should be a local truce in the Pas de Calais for a period of three years.

1439 had been a year of violent storms. One after another they swept across France during the summer. The harvest was ruined and wheat was so scarce that its prices soared, [15] while the failure of the wine vintage pushed the price up to 12d a gallon. In July, just as the Calais Conference was opening, John Talbot determined to go to the relief of Meaux, which was now the only town to the east of Paris still in English hands. It was being besieged by a strong force under Arthur de Richemont, liberally supported by cannons under Jean Bureau. Meaux had remained in English hands ever since Henry V had conducted his epic siege of it in 1422.

The town lay on the northern curve of a sharp bend in the River Marne, which was here about 70 yards wide and too deep to ford. The town itself was walled and moated, but across the river, and thus protected by it, lay the market along the south side of which ran a canal. The market was thus, in effect, an island into which the garrison had retreated. It was even more strongly defended than the town itself, which the French had occupied. Henry V had found that the town and market was the most obstinate target of his campaign. It had fallen to him eventually, but it was generally accepted that it was from the terrible epidemic which ravaged his men at Meaux that he himself contracted his final illness. Thus, for a whole variety of reasons, sentimental as well as tactical, Talbot felt that Meaux should not be allowed to fall without a blow being struck in its defence.

Accompanied by Somerset and Scales, and with some 3,000 men, he marched straight for the town. The prospect of fighting Arthur de Richemont, his enemy for so many years, no doubt appealed to him and, on arrival before the town, he sent his Herald forward with a formal challenge to individual combat.[16] De Richemont ignored it. Talbot then marched his small army back and forth in front of the town. There was still no response. His arrival had for all practical purposes turned the tables on the French. The besiegers were now the besieged. Using leather boats which he had brought with him, Talbot had no difficulty in passing both stores and reinforcements into the market. It was out of the question to take the town by assault, and he had to content himself with the sacking of a bastille on an island overlooking the market. Having put new heart into the garrison, Talbot had not the resources with which to do more. He had to bid them farewell and return to Rouen. Some weeks later, as no useful purpose could be served by holding out any longer, the garrison surrendered. It was a good example of the frustration which John Talbot was to suffer more and more as the years passed and the war became increasingly unpopular in the eyes of the English Government.

Meanwhile Talbot switched his attention to the recovery of towns in the Pays de Caux (between Rouen and Dieppe) which had been lost five years before. As soon as de Richemont had secured Meaux he had laid siege to Avranches, a town on the borders of Brittany and at the base of the Cotentin Peninsula. He had a siege army of about 6,000 men; at such a distance west of John Talbot's base, he could expect to be almost out of his reach, and if things went wrong, he could get help from his brother, the Duke of Brittany. In actual fact the latter had signed an agreement promising to support England, and he refused to give such help.

Warwick and Talbot decided that they should go to the relief of Avranches. The most that they could muster was 4,000 men. John Talbot arrived in the area in mid-December and approached the town from the north. Avranches is a beautiful town standing on an isolated hill half a mile south of the little River See, and four miles from the sea. The tidal waters are fordable in places and there are also some fords upstream of the town.

The French force was camped between the river and the town. John took up a position along the north bank of the river and for a few days he probed the position. He learned that de Richemont's undisciplined local mercenaries were in the habit of trickling away at night to find comfortable quarters in the nearby villages. He also discovered a ford upstream, of which de Richemont was apparently unaware, for it was quite unguarded.

On the night of December 22nd, John Talbot took his men round by the ford and, moving rapidly downstream, attacked the French camp. The sentries had no time to raise the alarm and there was practically no resistance. The army dispersed in panic and confusion and the English entered Avranches in triumph as dawn broke.

This episode had, however, an important sequel. De Richemont rode straight to Paris. There, in the rough terms which had made him so universally unpopular, he told King Charles that he could do nothing while he employed such an undisciplined rabble as soldiers. This encouraged the King in steps which he had already begun to take to reorganise and improve his army.

CHAPTER XI

THAT AUTUMN WARWICK, Margaret Talbot's father, died at Rouen and John lost yet another friend and supporter. The succession to his title raised difficulties. As Margaret was his eldest daughter and his heiress, she claimed that it devolved through her upon John Talbot. But James, Lord Berkeley maintained that, through his wife's connection with the Beauchamps, he and not Margaret was the proper heir. The law-suit over the Warwick inheritance which the Talbots initiated in 1440 was long and very bitter. It was not even settled at the time of Talbot's death. Hence arose his assumption, as expressed in his Will, that John Lisle would, in succession to himself, become Earl of Warwick. As events turned out he never did so.

The quarrel between the Talbots and the Berkeleys was not confined to the Law Courts. In 1440 John Lisle sent a process server named David Woodburne to Wootton to serve a sub-poena on Lord Berkeley. The latter retaliated by forcing the poor man to eat it, seals and all, before sending him back to Painswick. [1]

Finance was now a continuous source of worry to almost everyone from the King to the village herdsman. Government was extensively financed by loans. These took the form of advances of cash, or of enforced loans arising out of the Exchequer's failure to pay wages and salaries. In John's Will, referred to above, he directs his Executors to sue the King for such debts, so that they may have "my said debts in performing my Will". A council Mandate dated 3rd December 1440 [2] gives some indication of the method employed by the Exchequer on behalf of the King to ward of such importunate demands:

"Henry, by the Grace of God King of France and England, to our beloved and faithful the Treasurers and Governors-General of our finances in France and Normandy, greeting and love.

"We give you to know that, in consideration that for a certain time past our beloved and faithful cousin and Marshal of France, Lord de Talbot, has not had from us any charge as

116

Tomb of Richard, Earl of Warwick, at Warwick.
John and Margaret Talbot are shown among the 'weepers'.
(Photograph by John Wright Photography)

a Captain or Warden of Fortresses within our realm of France
or Duchy of Normandy and that at this present time he has
none from us except that of Lisieux and the custody of
Harfleur and Montivilliers which have been delivered to him
of late and immediately upon the surrender of the same into
our jurisdiction to hold until he shall have some other higher
and more ample provision we (to assist him in maintaining his
position in our service more honourably, to aid him in
supporting the charges which he must necessarily incur by
occasion of the same, and in order to retain him as oftentimes
has been done before this present day on this side of the sea in
our service), have appointed him to have and to take of us the
sum of 300 salus of gold for one quarter of a year beginning on
the Feast of St. Michael last past over and above the wages,

pension or estate of certain charges incident to the same estate which he receives from us.

"Wherefore we expressly command and enjoin you that, by our well beloved Pierre Baillé, Receiver General of our said finances, you cause to be paid and delivered out of the money by him received to the said Lord de Talbot or to his certain order the said sum of 111C. salus of gold or money to that amount at the rate of XXIXs. 111d. each (i.e. £438.15s.0d.) for the said quarter commencing at the said Michaelmas and upon the sole production of these presents and a sufficient acquittance all that which shall have been paid by the said Receiver on this account shall be allowed in his accounts and deducted from his receipts by our beloved and faithful accountants at Rouen whom we command so to do without any difficulty or delay.

"Dated at Rouen the III day of December in the Year of Grace One thousand four hundred and forty and of our reign the nineteenth.

"By the King at the relation of the Great Council." There follows the receipt which is dated 10th January 1441, and signed "R. Stafford".

In 1440 the political climate in England took a turn for the worse. Beaufort became even more outspoken in advocating peace with France. This roused Gloucester from his apathetic isolation and he drew up a lengthy document which he addressed to his nephew the King.[3] This was to the effect that certain eminent people were imposing on his youth; Gloucester attacked Beaufort in particular, inferring that his great wealth had been derived from the sale of offices. The Archbishop of York, who had also become a Cardinal, was included in the attack, which sweepingly condemned the whole foreign policy as unwise and corrupt, and appealed to the King to dismiss both Cardinals.[4]

Beaufort was unmoved. He raised yet again the proposal that Orleans who had now been captive for 25 years should be used to negotiate with King Charles, and he issued a manifesto explaining his reasons. It was about this time that Suffolk began to acquire more influence. He had been a singularly incompetent commander in France and he had turned his hand to political intrigue. He was on Beaufort's Council of State, together with Archbishop Kemp, Bishop Moleyns and the Earls of Huntingdon, Stafford and Northumberland. With the support of this Council Orleans' mission was duly arranged and he crossed to France. His ransom was set at around 400,000 Crowns[5] (i.e., about £70,000) of which 40,000 were to be paid down and the balance within six months of the Duke's release. Once again, if his efforts to secure peace were successful, King Henry would pay his expenses: if they were unsuccessful he was to return again to captivity. However, this plan coincided with a change of heart on the part of Burgundy who, now that he was in alliance with the French and at war with the English, offered to pay Orleans' ransom in full. The offer was accepted and Orleans, speaking better English than French,[6] returned at last to his own country.

The French, however, were not without their troubles. In the early months of 1440 the Dukes of Alençon and Bourbon, Dunois and the 16-year-old Dauphin, Louis, a cool astute youth who had a profound contempt for his father, led a revolt against the House of Valois. King Charles managed to suppress this powerful opposition but it was unfortunate that the English could not by then muster the resources to take advantage of the situation.

It was not until July 1440 that it was decided to capture Harfleur, at the mouth of the Seine, which had been in French hands for five years. A combined operation was planned, Somerset having command of the sea-borne force and John Talbot of the land. The garrison appealed to Charles for help and he sent a large army under de Richemont and La Hire (for once Xantrailles was not present) to its relief. John's force was only 1,000 strong but they set about the siege-works very thoroughly. Double lines of earthworks, circum- and contra-vallation were constructed instead of the usual isolated forts. The seaward approach was also defended, and indeed, the French did attack simultaneously from the sea, having eluded Somerset, and from the landward side. However, the English archers drove them off with heavy casualties. Incidentally, this must have meant withholding their fire until very close range, as plate armour had now been fully developed and arrows could only penetrate it at virtually, point-blank range. The French accepted defeat and fell back to Paris. In October John received the surrender of the garrison in Harfleur, referred to in the Council Mandate, dated December 3rd (vide p.116 above).

Following his suppression of the revolt against him, King Charles now assumed a more authoritative rôle and began to take a personal part in the conduct of operations. Encouraged by the capture of Creil, thanks largely to Bureau and his artillery, Charles now decided to recapture Pontoise. Throughout the war it was of great strategical importance and, now occupied by the English, it was a standing threat to Paris. The King decided to lead the attack himself.

He set up his headquarters on June 6th, 1441, at the Abbey of Maubuisson, two miles short of the river, and the siege began. [7] The bridge between the town and the south bank of the River Oise was in the hands of the garrison, with an earthworks on the far end of it. It was the bridge furthest down the river, which flows into the Seine a mere six miles downstream. Another bridge was therefore constructed a short distance downstream, opposite St. Martin's Abbey. A large bastille was erected enclosing the Abbey, and King Charles placed the Dauphin in command of it. Like the English before Orleans, Charles found that he had not enough men to occupy continuous lines of circumvallation round the town: a large gap existed to the north and east.

The strength of King Charles' army was put at about 5,000 men (Waurin estimates it at between ten and twelve thousand)[8] and nearly all his leading commanders were present, including La Hire and Xantrailles (together for the last time, as it turned out), de Richemont, Jean Bureau and a new arrival Sir Olivier de Cotiny, who was later to become Seneschal of Bordeaux. Bureau set to work to destroy the barbican at the outward end of the town's bridge and succeeded in doing so in a few days. But he also destroyed three arches of the bridge itself, thus rendering it useless for storming the town. His artillery made breaches in the walls from other directions, but each night the garrison succeeded in repairing them.

John Talbot was not inactive. He had sent two spies forward: both were in his pay as men-at-arms, but both were French born and could easily pass as villagers. They were Henry Amoure and Richard Vernon and they went first to Pontoise to examine the position and also to let Lord Clinton, the Captain of Pontoise, know that help would shortly be forthcoming. From there the two scouts went on to Conflans, where they mingled with the French soldiers. The report which they brought back to Talbot was comprehensive and he paid them well for their pains. (The Certificate for this payment, which also describes the duties performed by these two men, is to be seen in Appendix C.)

It seems likely that the appeal which the English Council at Rouen addressed to the King that same month was founded on the report of these men, and dictated by Talbot himself.[9] It reads:

"Our Sovereign Lord, we commend ourselves to you with all humility, subjection and true obedience which may it please you to know that although the advertisements, letters, persuasions, remonstrances and repeated discharges which we have often sent to your Majesty and to your noble Council in England, have not born fruit profitable and honourable to yourself and wholesome and necessary to us your poor servants and subjects in France. Still we write to you once more in extreme necessity, signifying that our malady is akin to exile or death and very close to total ruin.

"Matters stand so that little diligence or at least little effectual diligence has been employed in bestowing care and medecine to relieve the affliction and to cure the grievous sickness of this State which God has committed to you to govern. Thereby we perceive that the hearts of your subjects are cast down and enfeebled, much chilled and withdrawn from your love . . ." The letter continues on a reproving note, and informs the King that the French are making arrangements to lay siege to Pontoise with "a great body of troops who are wonderfully well provided with all kinds of necessaries". The letter concludes: "Lord Talbot is at Vernon waiting for all the troops that can be raised to go with him to do his best at the siege by God's help. Whatever diligence has been done or whatever commands have been issued in your name to any captains or troops by showing them your need they have indifferently obeyed. It is a great misfortune to you, our Sovereign Lord, that the said Lord Talbot has not a sufficient power for he has a high and notable desire to do the best he can for you against your said enemies. If . . ." (the manuscript ends here).

John Talbot was not optimistic about the effect which this forthright appeal might have, for on June 16th he marched off with about 4,000 men along the north bank of the Seine towards Pontoise, without waiting for a reply. [10]

Talbot's route took him close to the Abbey St. Martin, but its occupants did not offer to fight. Prisoners later told Talbot that this was on a direct order from the King and that the latter and de Richemont had strongly disagreed as to its wisdom. [11] In the event, therefore, Talbot was free to enter Pontoise, where he left all the stores and, at the cost of depleting his own force, some fresh men led by Scales and Fauconberg. He then returned the way he had come, taking wounded men with him, as far as Mantes, about 20 miles away. There he collected another supply train and repeated the manoeuvre a second time. But this time he was joined by York, with whom he had campaigned so successfully five years earlier, and who brought with him reinforcements that restored their combined strength to 2,000 or 3,000 men.

On the approach of the English King Charles now withdrew his army across the River Oise, leaving behind only the garrison in St. Martin's bastille under Cotiny. Yet again the relief train, now under York, was able to enter the town and deliver its supplies. Having done so, York and Talbot turned their offensive more directly against the French army.

York opened matters by sending his Herald, rather in the manner of Edward III, to inform King Charles that he intended to cross the River Oise with his army, whether the King liked it or not. [12] The effect of this was that Charles extended his army in a long defensive line all the way from where the Oise joins the Seine right up to Creil, a distance of some thirty miles.

York and Talbot now withdrew their men some ten miles to the north, where they were sure that Charles' scouts had lost touch with them. From there York took part of the army and marched rapidly to a point on the river Oise near Beaumont, 15 miles upstream from Pontoise. Making as much noise as possible, he attacked Beaumont while John Talbot pushed on still further north to a point opposite the Abbey of Royaumont. The river here was only some 30 yards wide, but it was unguarded. Using specially made leather boats Talbot's men were able to make a rapid crossing, and de Richemont found to his dismay that the English were once more on the same side of the river as himself. Only a few days earlier Charles' army had crossed the Oise from north to south; now he had to re-cross it from south to north to put it once more between himself and the English. When Talbot's men entered Maubuissen Abbey Charles' bed was still warm and his personal belongings lay everywhere in confusion. [13]

The French retreated south, aiming to place the River Seine between them and the English. King Charles took up his residence at Poissy, on the south bank of the Seine, and some fifteen miles south of Pontoise. The rapid marches of the various bodies of men were made even more exhausting by the stiflingly hot weather. Certainly the local French villagers were viewing the undignified game of hide-and-seek with amusement, and with some contempt for the part their King was playing. [14]

After crossing the Seine at Poissy, de Richemont posted a strong guard on the bridgehead, which made direct attack impossible. York and Talbot conferred as to how they could best come to grips with this elusive opponent. They evolved the following plan. John would take 1,000 men back to Mantes. He would cross the Seine there and, by a rapid night march, surprise the French at Poissy. They would undoubtedly retreat towards St. Denys, and to reach it would have to cross the Seine by a bridge slightly east of Conflans. Meanwhile York was to re-cross the Oise to its eastern bank at Neauville, and lie in wait for the French at their crossing. Thus, it was hoped, Talbot would drive them into a trap.

The whole success of this complicated manoeuvre depended on timing. The distance from Mantes to Poissy is 17 miles, and Talbot was expecting much from his men if they were to cover that distance in a night march and fight superior numbers at the end of it. They reached Poissy just as dawn was breaking and surprise was complete. Yet again the unfortunate French King found himself crossing the river to escape the English.

But unfortunately the trap failed to catch its prey. York over-estimated the time Talbot would take, and was too slow in reaching his position. He was just in time to see the French marching away across his front. However, Pontoise had been relieved. French morale had been severely shaken, and English morale had been revived: during July the besieged and the

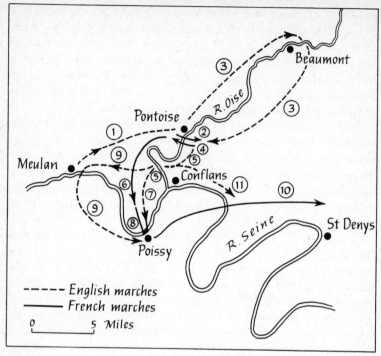

Seine et Oise Campaign

1. English enter Pontoise
2. French cross the Oise
3. English cross the Oise
4. French re-cross the Oise
5. English re-cross the Oise
6. French retreat to the Seine
7. English pursue to the Seine
8. French cross the Seine
9. Talbot crosses the Seine
10. French re-cross the Seine
11. York tries to intercept

(Reproduced from *The Agincourt War*, by Lieut. Col. Alfred H. Burne with permission of the publishers Eyre & Spottiswoode (Publishers) Ltd.)

besiegers exchanged long and most uncomplimentary ballads. [15] King Charles returned to Paris and York and John to Rouen. They were, however, criticised for not following up their tactical successes, but their wives and families remarked on their haggard appearance and exhaustion.

King Charles now showed his newfound strength of character. He remained determined to re-take Pontoise. The bridges were repaired, the guns were brought up again, and the town was once more invested, this time more completely. Yet again Talbot assembled a relieving force at Elboeuf and, on August 16th, 1441 he advanced along the direct road to Pontoise. Charles ordered de Richemont to advance to meet him. The two armies met at Vigny, nine miles west of Pontoise, but de Richemont did not attack or withdraw, nor did John wish to invite a battle. His object now was to get supplies into Pontoise. All day long the two armies sat watching each other. As night fell John ordered his men to light camp fires and to have a good meal. Going round he ordered them to make up their fires and then to join him a mile to the rear.

They moved off silently in the dark and marched away across the River Viosne, and then turned straight for Pontoise. As dawn broke they could see the French still in position and their own camp fires still smouldering. The river was between the two armies and John Talbot went down to its bank to wave his sword at the enraged de Richemont, who now could do nothing to prevent the relief of Pontoise.

On August 28th, Talbot reviewed the position of the beleaguered town: it had had a severe battering but morale was still high. On September 6th he made a fifth relieving expedition and, this time, it was clear that the defences had been so weakened that, although they were not short of provisions, the garrison must soon be overwhelmed by the sheer weight of the French numbers.

The assault came only ten days later, and it was overwhelming. The garrison fought to the last; one man, it was said, even fighting from beneath the belly of King Charles' horse, under which he had ducked for protection. About 500 men were killed; the remainder, including their gallant commander, Lord Clinton, were put to ransom.

The loss of Pontoise was a grievous blow. It showed that, although the English could defeat the French in battle, victory was useless unless England was prepared to provide the resources which would sustain her position in France. It was becoming increasingly apparent that the new regime in England was not prepared to do that. On the contrary, the Duke of Orleans, who was still trying to negotiate peace terms, was now having some success. King Charles himself had led an army south into Gascony, probably with the object of aiding the negotiations by leaving the field clear in the north. Almost the only further action of the year was La Hire's siege of La Réole. The town held out through the autumn and on into the winter, which proved to be another hard one. The French soldiers suffered severely and John Talbot's old opponent, La Hire, literally froze to death.

The lull in the war allowed John and Margaret Talbot to visit England. John's exploits, including the comical Pontoise campaign, had fired the public's imagination and, in addition, he was now almost the sole survivor of the old days of England's glory under King Hal. John Talbot had, in fact, become a national hero and he received an enthusiastic welcome.

Talbot had indeed made the French look foolish at a time when England's affairs were in a poor state; but his popularity also stemmed from the fact that it was universally recognised that he stood aloof from the sordid political struggle which was dominating English public life. At a time when, unfortunately, the support of most men could be bought at a price, his considerable influence was not for sale. The devotion which he inspired at all levels is also apparent. Without it no commander could have asked as much of his men as Talbot did: it was a devotion which lived on in the hearts of many, both French and English, for years after his death, and which was ultimately recorded by Shakespeare.

It was thus a highly popular gesture when early in 1442 the King conferred an Earldom on Talbot. He decided at first to take Salop as his title, but changed it almost at once to Shrewsbury. Blackmere, in Shropshire, had figured largely in his life. He was descended from the Montgomerys, ancient Earls of Whitchurch, [16] which is also in Shropshire, and his personal bodyguard was drawn from there. He had indicated, when he lay wounded at Patay, that it was at Whitchurch that he wished to be buried.

CHAPTER XII

INEVITABLY ATTEMPTS were made to drag John Talbot, or Shrewsbury as he should now be styled, into the political arena. Many of those engaged in it were ageing, and he himself was now in his sixtieth year, or older. Beaufort was on the point of retiring from his Bishopric, and the reins of power which Henry VI's weak hands refused to grasp were falling more and more into those of the ambitious Earl of Suffolk.

Gloucester might have withstood Suffolk's policies in years gone by, but now he too was ageing and was increasingly absorbed in his patronage of, and researches into, the world of art and literature. He was the first English patron of the Italian Renaissance, in which the Shrewsburys were also deeply interested.[1] The Duke had, some years earlier, commissioned Zano Castiglione, Bishop of Bayeux (a town under Talbot's jurisdiction) to go to Italy to buy books. Those he brought back ranged from Bruni's translation of Aristotle's *Politics,* and Latin translations of Plato, Ptolemy and Plutarch, to a vellum folio of a medical treatise by the Arabian surgeon Aboo-1-Kassim. Engrossed in such matters, Gloucester now paid the minimum attention to national politics, especially since his intervention two years earlier had had little effect.

Meanwhile the Shrewsburys had domestic matters which needed their attention, chief among which was reform of the system of land tenure, and the local rights of people living on their land. They found, as they journeyed round Goodrich, Painswick, Whitchurch, Worksop, Sheffield and other Manors, that there was an urgent need to remedy injustices which were part of the old feudal system. Their treatment of the Manor of Painswick will serve as an example of their reforms.[2]

As one of a series of investigations Shrewsbury ordered an inquest to be held there on April 21st, 1442, which he personally found time to attend. He addressed certain questions to the Jury, and directed that their findings should be communicated to him. The result was a thorough reform of the administration of the Manor, framed in the spirit of a benevolent landlord instead of a feudal overlord.

The first article remedied a serious injustice with which the Shrewsburys were particularly concerned. Widows, having lost their husbands fighting in France had previously forfeited their tenements to their next of kin. Further, they had had to pay heriots to the Lord of the Manor.* Yet the loss of their husbands had given them no right to marry again. Thus, deprived of their house and their means of livelihood, they inevitably became destitute. Shrewsbury did away with this scandalous state of affairs and allowed them to marry again.

The Inquest also made many recommendations with regard to local law, as to pasturing on common lands and on the waste lands of the Manor. Villagers could previously purchase licences to fatten their geese, pigs, cattle and horses on such land, and heavy fines had been levied for doing so without a licence. Talbot now abolished such licensing. He also relinquished all interest, as Lord of the Manor, in the Rep Tax, the payment for reaping by man, woman or child. He ordered too that each man should have for his own use a portion of arable land, the best at 12d per annum, the second at 8d, the third at 6d, the fourth at 4d, and the worst land at 2d per annum. These were but a few of the many respects in which John and Margaret Shrewsbury improved the lot of village people on their land.

Their accommodation in London was now confined to the Talbot Inn in Whitechapel, for the Furnival Inn in Holborn was, by then, fully occupied by the Exchequer Clerks. (3) It was soon to be linked to Gray's Inn as one of the first of the Inns of Court.

Richard Talbot, still Archbishop of Dublin, an office he held until he died in August 1449, crossed the sea to meet the Shrewsburys. The Irish Parliament had asked him to lay various requests before the King. There was the inevitable request for money, and the equally inevitable complaint about the Earl of Ormond that he "is aged, unwieldy and unlusty for labour, for he hath, for lack of labour, lost in substance all his castles, towns and lordships that he had. Wherefore it is unlikely that he will conquer more land for you, the King. Moreover he hath made Irishmen, grooms and pages of his

---

*Heriot was a payment (which could be made in live or dead stock or in cash) on decease of a tenant.

household, Knights of the Shire."[4] The discord between the rival factions in Ireland continued unabated.

Talbot's respite from service was very brief. The King, or rather Suffolk speaking for him, told him that he was to take soldiers back with him to France as soon as possible. Talbot apparently pointed out that soldiers required paying and that the King was already in his debt for over £20,000. The following Mandate is dated 12th May, 1442:[5] "Henry etc., etc., . . . For as much as for the setting over the sea of our cousin the Lord Talbot and of the army that shall go in his company . . . there is great need for haste and for large sums of money of which we now have none, nor cannot have without the taxing of our subjects or sale and parting with some of our jewels. And in so far as the tax which we can levy at this time for the said cause will not suffice for the contenting of the said army in ready money, and that we would not for our peace and that of our true subjects. . . . we direct therefore and charge you that, on receipt of these presents, you do pawn as many of our jewels as to cover the payments made by you for the army and payments made by us amounting to £15,000 due unto our cousin the Duke of York, Lieutenant General and Governor of our realm of France and Duchy of Normandy and as far as the said jewels will stretch if you can do it. And these presents shall be your sufficient warrant and discharge. Given under our Privy Seal at our Castle of Windsor, the 18th day of May the 20th year of our reign."

In fact only about 1,000 marks (£700) were raised on October 12th, and Beaufort added plate, on loan to the King, valued at £4,000, although it was widely known that the King was already in his debt for over £170,000 in an ever escalating figure which was to exceed £200,500 when Beaufort died five years later.

The Shrewsburys returned to France in the late summer of 1442, with a puny little force of 1,000 men. Nevertheless John captured Conches in Normandy and then made a typically sudden, unexpected, attack on Dieppe. Realising that he could not take it by assualt, he constructed a bastille overlooking the port, and put his bastard son, Henry, "a valiant young man" in command of it with a garrison of 600 men. He himself went on to Rouen, where he took up the office and duties of Constable of France. The French, "quickly advertised" of this, sent no less a general that Dunois with 15,000 men to relieve Dieppe. After a fierce little action of three days, at the end of which they ran out of powder and arrows, [6] Henry had to capitulate, to the "great displeasure" of his father [7] who, nevertheless, ransomed him at once.

During the autumn and winter of 1442 the Beaufort party finally achieved complete power in England. The way this came about was, curiously enough, through an attack, not on Gloucester, the figurehead of the opposition, but on his wife Eleanor, Oldcastle's widow. She was accused of practising witchcraft. At her trial references were made to Gloucester's interest in astrology, and it was hinted that he too might have been implicated. Eleanor was found guilty and sentenced to do a most ignominious and degrading penance through the streets of London. This disgrace had its expected effect on Gloucester, who retired into an even closer seclusion, leaving Richard of York as the sole opposition to the House of Lancaster in the persons of Suffolk and Somerset, Beaufort's nephews.

As if to mark this superiority, Suffolk arranged the appointment of Somerset to command an army destined to go to Gascony to relieve that Province from French attack. He was given the resounding title of Captain General of Gascony, which was in itself a slight to the Duke of York whose authority as King's Lieutenant covered, theoretically, the whole of France. Somerset, with an army of about 7,000 men, landed at Cherbourg in August 1443. Nobody seemed to know why he had done this instead of sailing to Bordeaux, but it may have been that he feared to prolong the voyage. He was not in good health and certainly did not relish any form of hardship. From Cherbourg he marched south along the border between Maine and Brittany. At Shrewsbury's headquarters in Rouen, they wondered where he was going and hoped that his advent might serve some useful purpose.

It was not to be. Somerset captured La Guerche, a town in Brittany, which was stupid in the extreme as the Duke was in treaty with England. In any case the town had no strategic value. Somerset then handed it back to Brittany and moved rather aimlessly through Maine. It was said that when one of his Captains asked him what his plan was he replied: "I do not divulge my secrets to anyone. If even my shirt knew my secrets

I would burn it." That winter he returned to England and died shortly afterwards. He was succeeded by his brother, Edmund.

Somerset's absurd activities demonstrated the inadequacy of direction from Westminster, and created even greater despondency amongst the English in France. The task of maintaining some semblance of English authority was becoming almost impossible, and it requires little imagination to picture the frustration, irritation and sorrow which assailed a man of Shrewsbury's efficiency and patriotic vigour. At that time several Princes were raising men for a crusade against the Turks in Walachia. The demand for English commanders, and particularly for English archers, was high, and Talbot lost some good men. Had he himself been a younger man he might well have joined them.

Meanwhile King Henry had now reached the age of twenty-one and the question of finding him a Queen was becoming important. After some abortive explorations, his choice fell on Princess Margaret of Anjou, the beautiful fifteen-year-old daughter of the King of Sicily. As the talented daughter of a titular though completely impoverished Sovereign, she seemed to be entirely qualified to marry the King of England. But, even more significantly, her aunt was Queen of France and her father one of the King's most intimate advisers. Henry instructed Suffolk to open negotiations with King Charles.

Closely linked with this, and probably uppermost in Suffolk's mind, was the question of peace. He saw it as an opportunity which had to be seized at almost any price. The only dissentient voice in the Council of State was that of Gloucester, in whose view peace was a betrayal of English interests. But, since his wife's disgrace, his opposition counted hardly at all.

Suffolk crossed to France in March 1444, and a Conference took place at Montils-les-Tours on the River Loire. But difficulties arose. Charles held all the cards in the shape of armed strength, military initiative, the well-known desire for peace on the part of the English Government, and the prize of a highly desirable bride for the English King. He was determined to exact a high price.

The point at which the negotiations ran into difficulties was not, as hitherto, the English claim to complete sovereignty over France. Weakly, as it appeared to those of the older generation, Suffolk was prepared to barter that sovereignty for the absolute possession of Normandy. This time it was the old question of homage which arose. It had lain dormant for eighty-four years; now Charles, from his new position of strength, demanded that Henry should do homage for Gascony and Normandy. On that point even Suffolk would not give way and negotiations broke down. Instead, a two years' truce was agreed, and Suffolk turned to negotiations solely concerned with Princess Margaret.

As it was known that her father could not pay a dowry, it was hardly discussed and the matter of her marriage to King Henry appeared to be quickly and satisfactorily settled to the mutual satisfaction of all concerned. Suffolk returned somewhat triumphantly to England and created himself a Duke and Marquis in recognition of his services to the King. There was some talk of secret clauses in the marriage contract, and even of personal benefits received by Suffolk, but nothing marred the celebrations on both sides of the Channel which marked the opening of the truce on 27th June, 1444.

As Constable of France it fell to Talbot's lot to arrange the ceremonial espousal of Princess Margaret, in Rouen Cathedral, on March 22nd, 1445. During the course of these preparations the Shrewsburys had frequent contact with her, and a close friendship developed between them despite their wide difference in age. It was forty-six years since the young John Talbot had witnessed the unhappy departure from France of Princess Isabella to become Richard II's Queen. Princess Margaret was slightly more mature but almost as unhappy, and so impoverished that she had to borrow clothes and money from the Shrewsburys. After the most impressive ceremony, at which Suffolk stood proxy for the King, he conducted her across the Channel with a considerable train which included the Shrewsburys. They sailed from Dieppe on April 8th and encountered such a savage storm that it was thirty-six hours before they landed at Porchester. The Princess was so ill that Suffolk had to carry her ashore. There she borrowed a crown piece (3s.4d.) from Margaret Shrewsbury to give to the Church as a thank-offering for her safe arrival.

She was married to Henry VI at Titchfield Abbey, by the

Bishop of Salisbury, on April 22nd. The Shrewsburys gave her an illuminated manuscript which is now in the British Library. The title page represents the Queen with King Henry, surrounded by their Court, receiving the book from Shrewsbury. It is "a surviving monument to his exquisite taste in the fine arts".[8] The Royal Seal fills up a rich oriel, with vaulted ceiling, grained and painted blue with gold stars. With Shrewsbury is one of the dogs which he had trained to accompany him everywhere, acting as both guard dogs and hounds. The original Talbot Dogs, which have passed into Heraldic History, are said to have come from Dalmatia.

The entry of the King and Queen into London on May 28th was a triumph for both her and for Suffolk, and the Coronation took place on May 30th, amid great rejoicing. The King was quite intoxicated by the beauty of his Queen, and, in spite of the poor state of his finances, he spared no expense. So it came about, in this euphoric atmosphere, that she persuaded him to make public the secret clause to which Suffolk had agreed at Tours. It was no less than the cession to the French of Maine and Anjou.

As soon as this became known a storm burst round Suffolk's head, and the unfortunate young Queen's popularity evaporated overnight. Great pressure was put on Gloucester, York and Shrewsbury to take steps to renounce the Treaty, but they were not prepared to precipitate civil war. The anger as well as the hardship that this caused, particularly to the English residents in Maine of whom there were many, was forcefully addressed to Henry.[9] They petitioned not only for adequate compensation, but for justice to be done to the "persons who thus wickedly and unfaithfully counselled you".

In the first week of July 1445 an Embassy landed unexpectedly at Dover. It appeared that its members represented King Charles, the King of Spain, the King of Sicily (Queen Margaret's father), and the Dukes of Brittany and Alençon. No-one had a clear idea as to the exact object of this imposing cavalcade, which was so large that towns on its route to London could not accommodate it, and it had to be divided into two parties. Slowly they made their way towards London, while messengers galloped to and fro between them and Suffolk.[10] Dorset and Shrewsbury, accompanied by a large number of knights, met them a league down river from

London Bridge, and the bridge itself was lined by the Trades, each Trade being dressed uniformly and richly. The Lord Mayor was waiting to greet the party as it entered the city. The members of the Embassy, who had been apprehensive as to whether their reception would be friendly or hostile, were suitably impressed, and Suffolk no doubt felt that, as a result of all his hard work, a peace agreement might still be possible.

The next day, July 15th, Suffolk, Dorset and Shrewsbury went to fetch the members of the Embassy by water to Westminster and to escort them to the King. He greeted them rather shyly, perched on a high stool and dressed in a long robe of red and gold cloth, and doffing his cap to the prelates of the party.[11] He kept darting defiant looks at his uncle Gloucester on his left, and smiling affectionately at Suffolk on his right, even reaching out to clutch him by the hand occasionally. There was a brief exchange of formalities, after which, Dorset, Salisbury and Shrewsbury escorted the Embassadors back to their lodgings. The next day, when Dorset and Shrewsbury arrived at the appointed time for their escort duty, they were surprised to find Suffolk already there and in deep discussion with the Ambassadors. Indeed, as they were led towards the room occupied by the Embassy, they clearly heard Suffolk saying emphatically: "I am a servant of the King of France and, with the exception of my master the King of England, I will serve him with my body and my goods against the whole world".[12] It was clear that Suffolk's part in the arrival of the Embassy, in the lavish welcome which it received (in which Shrewsbury, the popular war hero, was seen to be taking an active part), and in the negotiations themselves, was highly suspect. Suffolk arranged for the Ambassadors to be taken to visit the ageing Cardinal Beaufort, recently returned from Rome; they were shown the home of the Carmelites (the White Friars) in Fleet Street, and of the Grey Friars in Newgate Street; the Tower, Westminster Abbey and other places of interest, in an effort to encourage their desire for peace. Yet nothing would move the French from their determination that the King of England should pay homage to the King of France for Gascony and Normandy, and now, in addition, for Querain, Périgord, Calais and Juynes. Suffolk, Somerset and the King himself indicated that they saw no objection, but, perhaps surprisingly, Beaufort would have none of it; the remaining Members of the Council supported the strong opposition of York and Shrewsbury. Gloucester refused even to meet the Embassy.

The negotiations finally broke down on July 31st, and the Embassy departed. This was a severe set-back for Suffolk and increased his unpopularity. Nevertheless he and Somerset still largely controlled the King and Queen, and, as the months passed, the influence of the King declined and that of the Queen increased. Nevertheless she was a mere girl, and Suffolk began to realise that she was not going to be strong enough to protect him and that he was fighting for his life. In 1446 he persuaded the Queen to send York to France and Shrewsbury once more to Ireland. [13]

Although it was twenty-seven years since his previous period as Viceroy, there were many in Dublin who still remembered Talbot. He and his brother, the Archbishop, had become almost legendary figures. The latter died on the 15th August, 1449, and was buried in St. Patrick's Church before the steps of the Altar, under an ornate marble monument. [14]

The Patriotic Party were by now in a commanding position in the country districts. The common Englishry accepted the leadership of the Anglo-Irish Earls who, with the Gaelic Chieftains playing a considerable part, were building up an effective native rule. The English government could not hope to counter this. [15] Yet that was what Talbot was now being asked to do. He had outlived most of his contemporaries and was no longer in the prime of life. But, as before, he made numerous marches into hostile territory, going as far as Youghal in the south west and along the coast of Waterford. It was all enemy territory now, and very different from the subservient, if sullen, country through which he had marched with Richard II forty-seven years earlier. The Le Poers, the Geraldines, the Burkes and others, who had done homage to the King, were now the opposing leaders.

As usual Talbot received no financial support from the Crown, but he was created Earl of Wexford and Waterford and Baron of Dungarvan, and granted the largely fictitious rights of the wreck of the sea from Youghal to Waterford. [16] This privilege was somewhat hollow as the County of Waterford was "not at this time amenable to the jurisdiction of the English Crown". [17] He was also appointed Seneschal and Constable of Ireland.

He found that it was now impossible, by language, by dress or by countenance, to distinguish between "loyal settlers", "English rebels" or even "Irish enemies". The passage of years and much intermarriage had eradicated differences which had been apparent at the turn of the century. To remedy this, Talbot persuaded Parliament, when it met at Trim in January 1447, to pass a Bill to the effect that all who wished to be taken for Englishmen must shave their upper lip at least every other week; otherwise it would be assumed that they were Irish. The Bill also decreed that sons of labourers must follow their father's calling, as had been the case in England for many years.

Plundering and looting had been so widespread for so long that all sorts and conditions of men now possessed accoutrements normally worn only by knights or nobles. Talbot ordered that, in future, only knights or prelates of the Church might use gilt bridles, harness and accoutrements, and that it was a punishable offence for anyone else to do so. But Talbot was first and foremost a soldier, who could scatter armies and bring rebels to heel. He had not the constructive genius required for the difficult office of Viceroy, of which he was the last who strove to keep England's colony in Ireland true to the English tradition by force of arms. [18]

It was while Talbot was thus engaged in Ireland, and York in France, that Suffolk decided to bring matters to a head with regard to Gloucester. The latter had, by now, no real interest outside his library and it would seem that he could well have been left to enjoy his old age. Nevertheless he was summoned to attend Parliament, at Bury St. Edmunds, to hear certain charges against him. Simultaneously a rumour spread that he was about to lead a revolt against the King. This provided sufficient excuse for Suffolk to assemble a force of no fewer than 40,000 men, nominally to protect the Members of Parliament.

Gloucester arrived at Bury on 18th February, 1447, accompanied by a mere 80 men, which was his normal retinue. On arrival he was arrested and, most ignominiously, guarded by two Yeomen and a Sergeant, his own servants being removed. Three days later he was dead. In spite of Suffolk's efforts to contradict the rumour, it was widely believed that he died of poison. He was buried equally ignominiously in the Abbey of the Grey Friars at Babwell, and another of the great names associated with Henry V disappeared from the stage. His books are held in what was then the new Bodleian Library in Oxford.

Suffolk's unpopularity became even more pronounced, and his part in Gloucester's death, whether it was by poisoning or by a stroke, undoubtedly hastened the fate which later befell him. Gloucester's death was followed within a matter of weeks by that of his old enemy, Cardinal Beaufort, and England was virtually ruled by Suffolk, Somerset and the young Queen. For no very apparent reason they brought York back from France and sent him to Dublin in place of Talbot. The latter, now over sixty-four, was, however, not allowed to remain idle. He was required once again to cross the Channel, with Edmund Duke of Somerset (who had now succeeded his brother John), as Marshal of France. It was in that capacity that his signature appears on the receipt, the translation of which reads as follows:

"We John, Count Shrewsbury of Wexford and Waterford, Lord Talbot of Furnival and Strange, Marshal of France, acknowledge receipt from Jehan le Brasseur, Supervisor of Reliefs and Taxes at Falaise, the sum of five hundred Touraine pounds which sum he had been commanded by the Treasurer and General Collector of Normandy to pay us by virtue of the order given at Rouen on the second day of the present month of April. This sum we hold for our Lord, the King, in quittance from the aforesaid Collector and all others. Witness our hand and seal the twelfth day of the said month of April before Easter in the year 1448.

(signed) Talbot"

Although the text gives Shrewsbury his full title, he signs it, perhaps rather laboriously, but simply as "Talbot"

Detail of receipt
showing Talbot's signature

The truce, meanwhile, was rapidly deteriorating into sporadic warfare and the balance of military power now lay more heavily than ever in favour of the French.

King Charles had at last become skilled in the arts of war, and an authoritative and decisive ruler. His army, now composed of professional soldiers, was efficient and its artillery, under Jean Bureau, was far in advance of any other army in the world. The English, on the other hand, were reduced to numerous small garrisons and could not muster an army of any effective size to take the field. Even the garrisons themselves were unreliable. Men who had fought gallantly in years gone by had settled into their routine duties, and many had married local girls. They had become so much part of the community that they were indistinguishable from their French neighbours, whose views and interests they now shared. It was no wonder that security was far from sure.

Nevertheless in spite of the weakness of their position, Suffolk and Somerset both talked and acted as if England's old supremacy still existed. They also encouraged a form of bandit warfare which was quite contrary to the rules of chivalry under which Talbot had always fought. A meeting was arranged between French and English envoys at Louviers to end this guerilla warfare. The French alleged that the English in Mantes, Verneuil, and Loenguy were waylaying travellers on the road to Orleans, robbing them and cutting their throats. Much the same allegations were made about the garrisons of Neufchatel, Gournay and Gerberoy, whose men were said to operate in disguise on the road between Paris and Amiens. The French demanded a cessation of this brigandage, an exchange of towns recently captured, and payment of compensation to the Duke of Brittany for damage done in an attack on his town of Fougères. [19] The English refused these peremptory demands and the English envoys left abruptly, doing considerable damage to Louviers as they departed. Somerset wrote to Charles complaining about this and demanding £800 for the damage done. Within a few days open hostilities were resumed.

Talbot, in his capacity of Marshal of France, wrote to Henry reporting this, and told the King that they would have to fight to retain any French possessions at all. He asked him to provide the means with which to do so. He added rather pointedly that the Burghers of Rouen were now his only sound supporters. He sent this appeal, and one written by the City Council, to England by his Master of the Ordnance, William

Gloucester. On 12th May, 1449, the King replied as follows:[20]

"Very dear and faithful cousin and our very dear and well-beloved liegemen,

"We have received your letters written at our city of Rouen on the eleventh day of April last and sent to us by William Gloucester the Master of our Ordnance in the Duchy of Normandy, containing credence with certain articles delivered to us. Which credence and articles we have heard and given good heed to the matters contained in these articles to which we have given an answer and made provision for some of them as our very dear and faithful cousin the Earl of Suffolk and the said William who are duly informed in the said matters and who are at this time coming to your said city can inform you. Wherefore our will is and we command you that to our said cousin and the said William you will give faith and credence in regard to what they shall tell you from us touching the articles above said.

"And may our Lord have you always in His holy keeping

Henry R."

Feeling possibly that this empty response was a little inadequate, the King wrote a second letter the following day, addressing himself more specifically to the people of Rouen:[21]

"Dear and Well-beloved liegemen we salute you often.

"And as by the information of our very dear and faithful cousin, John Lord Talbot, we are credibly informed that in the protection of our right and the preservation of our true and loyal subjects of our town of Rouen and the neighbourhood, you have had and taken great pains and diligence in keeping them in our obedience to the great honour and profit of us and the discomforture of our enemies, for which we thank you with our whole heart, praying you always to continue thus towards us.

"Knowing that we have at this time made provision for you and for our other said lieges and subjects there, and so from time to time we will provide, if it please God, in such manner that you will be shortly comforted as our very dear and faithful Cousin, the Earl of Suffolk and William Gloucester, Master of our Ordnance in our said Duchy, who for this cause has diligently interceded with us and our Council in England, who are now coming to you, will know how to tell you more fully from us.

"And may our Lord have you always in His holy keeping.

Dated 13th May 1449

To Richard Cuesone, Lieutenant of Rouen

and John Salveyn, Knight, Bailly there.

Henry R."

William of Worcester's *Annales* quotes[22] the following document as being in circulation during the summer of 1449. It is unsigned, but appears to have been written by a person with very detailed knowledge of overall administration and, as it refers to the Duke of Somerset as "this Somerset" by a person of considerable standing. It is written in French and is described as "Suggestions for questions to be asked of the Duke of Somerset regarding his administration in France".

"1. Let it be asked of the Duke of Somerset by the Council of the King how much money he has had from the taking of Fougères and why he gave permission to Sir Francis L'Arragonnoys to take the said town.

"2. Let him be asked why he recognised those persons who made the said capture and why he caused troops to be put within the said fortress and why he forbade the said Sir Francis that for his life he should not surrender it whatever might be the letters which the Duke might send."

(Points 3 and 4 continue in the same vein)

"5. Let the said Somerset be asked what money he promised when he was at the Palace of Rouen, to Menypeny (Sir William Moneypeny) if he would attend to his interests in some matters he wanted done with the Lords upon the part of France and what were these matters. And if Sir Thomas Hoo who was then Chancellor of Normandy were closely questioned he would have much to say upon this affair.

"6. There are due by this said Somerset large sums of money from the wages of the soldiers who he would not pay, so that it became necessary for them to plunder the people and to waste the countryside and this to continue to such an extent that there was none that dared continue in the country who was not either killed or plundered . . . as he would do no justice to the inhabitants it followed that the whole country turned to the French.

"7. Let Lord de Gray, the Master of the Bailly of Rouen, be

required upon oath to state all that he has formerly heard told to the said Bailly of Rouen his prisoner and let this be done in the presence of all the Lords of the Council and let him not fail to tell the truth for any man in the world whomsoever he may be.

"8. Let Somerset be asked what money he has given to those who were in the County of Maine for the compensation which they ought to have . . . of which money he has given none but has applied it to his own private advantage. And in this matter it would be well to speak to Mundeford who was then at Le Mans on his account to whom the said money was given in part to be delivered to the said Somerset."

This was part of an attack on Somerset which culminated in a Bill being laid before the Parliament of November 1450 naming some twenty-nine persons, headed by Somerset, who, it was asserted, had been "misbehaving about the King's Royal person". It was all part of the great division between York and Lancaster but it sadly reflects also the depths to which the English administration in France had sunk. It is so completely alien to everything for which Talbot had stood for nearly half a century that it emphasises, too, the gulf which existed between him, as Marshal of France, and Somerset as the King's Lieutenant. His own position remained clear. King Henry VI was the lawful Sovereign whom he must continue to serve as he had served three predecessors before him. Each of them had grave faults. Richard II had squandered English wealth and brought the Crown into disrepute. Henry IV had failed to unite the country behind him. Henry V, by his absolute determination to recover what he regarded as his lost inheritance, had laid on England's shoulders a burden which succeeding generations had found too heavy to carry. Henry VI, by his supine ineffectiveness, was now bringing England to the very verge of civil war. It was not for Talbot to vary his degree of service according to the merits of the King whom he served, and for him to denounce Somerset would be of no service to England. Suffolk and Queen Margaret would ensure that Somerset did not suffer eclipse.

Any question of retirement was, however, abruptly taken out of Talbot's hands when, in July of that year (1449) the French King declared that, as England had broken the truce, it no longer existed. He despatched four columns into Lower

Normandy which converged on it from the east, south and west. The English Headquarters in Rouen could do nothing but watch as town after town, garrison after garrison fell to the French attack. Coutances, Gisors, Castell, Galliard, Ponteau-de-Mère, (the medieval spelling of "Pont Audemer" the bridge that Audemer built) Saint Lo, Festampe, Neucastell, Argenton, Lisieux; all these fell by yielding rather than by siege, and in several others the townspeople rose against their English garrisons and declared their allegiance to King Charles. Many Captains of towns "returned to England and died of grief of heart in very great poverty". [23] These were sad days for Talbot. All the labours and ambitions of Henry V, Bedford, Salisbury and hundreds upon hundreds of brave men were swept away in a matter of weeks, and he had to stand by and watch it happen.

CHAPTER XIII

TALBOT TOOK ALL the steps he could to prevent Rouen falling to the French, either by attack or by betrayal from within. He organised wall defences, and also strict patrols with power to seize any citizen who seemed to be acting suspiciously. At the beginning of October his scouts told him that Charles had set up his headquarters at Louviers, and a few days later a deputation appeared at the city gates summoning Rouen to surrender. Talbot angrily told the man on duty at the gate to turn them away. [1] a second deputation appeared, and again, without consulting Somerset, Talbot sent them away. A column encamped at Pont de l'Arche was commanded by Talbot's old enemy, Dunois, and it was he who was now ordered by the King to take Rouen by storm.

The weather was atrocious, and Dunois' men made a rather half-hearted attack on the walls through gales and heavy rain. Dunois hoped that this would spark off an insurrection inside the city, and it might well have done so for there was much disaffection among the citizens. But the strict patrols worked well, and Dunois withdrew his men to Pont de l'Arche. Shrewsbury's watchfulness had not, however, been entirely successful. Someone managed to get out of the city and report to Dunois that French sympathisers had possession of part of the walls between two towers.

On hearing this the King took personal command and led the army back to Rouen. They took up position on two sides of the city: one force, under Dunois, between Chartons and Rouen, and one, under Lord de Jallonges, outside the Beauvais Gate. On Thursday, 16th October Dunois' force attacked the walls where the traitors were, and, naturally gained a footing. It says much for Talbot's organisation that he saw the danger at once. With his Herald carrying his standard and his bodyguard around him he personally led the counter-attack which drove the French off the walls with heavy casualties. [2] In the lull which followed, crowds of citizens milled around Talbot, cheering him, and even Somerset came personally to congratulate him.

But his triumph was short-lived. The following day one of

the Cathedral officials, Richard Olivier, escaped from the city and returned with a document, signed personally by King Charles, giving safe conduct to the Archbishop of Rouen and certain Lords and Esquires enabling them to leave the City to negotiate, on behalf of the City Council, the terms on which Rouen would make its submission to Charles. Talbot had neither means nor authority to prevent such negotiations and the English garrison would not, in any event, be bound by the terms agreed upon even if the City Council ratified them. Talbot therefore had to allow them to leave for their rendez- vous with Dunois at Pont de Saint Ouen. They were absent all day and it was late at night when, having reached aggreement as to how the city should be handed over, they arrived back. By that time it was too late for them to gain entry and they had to spend a cold, wet and uncomfortable night outside the city walls. [3] However, early the next morning, Saturday 18th October, 1449, the Archbishop called a meeting of the townsfolk in the Town Hall and announced that they had reached complete agreement with the French; he added that they should all be happy to have received grace and pardon from the King of France for all their offences. He promised that no citizen would suffer loss.

Talbot promptly ordered all the English, including Somerset and his family, into the Castle, where he was determined to fight it out to a finish. The next day, Sunday, the citizens opened the city gates to the French and, from the Citadel, Talbot watched them take up position round the Castle. Somerset now took matters into his own hands and asked to negotiate with King Charles, who had moved into the Monastery of Saint Catherine, overlooking the city from outside the Martainville Gate. Somerset asked for a revision of the terms of surrender which had been negotiated by the City Burghers. The King coldly replied that, as the English had taken no part in them, new negotiations would be required, and that, before he could allow the English to go, he would require their agreement to surrender Honfleur, Harfleur, and many other places in the Pas de Calais. Somerset returned, crestfallen, to the Citadel, and he and Talbot and the leading captains argued far into the night. It is not difficult to imagine how the argument ran.

On October 24th, Dunois offered that, if Somerset and

Talbot would surrender the Citadel and make themselves prisoners with a further eighteen hostages, King Charles would give everybody else safe conduct to Calais: there were various other suggestions also, but all were dependent on the surrender within fifteen days of Honfleur, Harfleur, Caudebec, Montevilliers and Tancarville. This meant the virtual evacuation by the English of the whole of Normandy, and, to do Somerset justice, he was not at that stage prepared to agree to such a drastic step. Sir Thomas Hoo acted as intermediary and, through him, they told the King that his terms were unacceptable. Nevertheless the argument inside the Citadel continued and next day negotiations resumed.

The French were, of course, in a position to dictate any terms they liked, and their only concession was to agree that Somerset, his wife and children and his men, should all have safe conduct to leave France. But they must take nothing with them: all artillery and prisoners were to be left behind and 50,000 Salus of Gold (approximately £73,000) were to be paid to King Charles within a year's time. There was also provision for payment to the citizens of Rouen of what was said to be owing to them. [4] All the towns and fortresses in the Pays de Caux were to be surrendered. But, having arrived at this penal agreement, the French then made it clear that they did not trust Somerset, Suffolk or the English regime to abide by it. They pointed to the way the truce terms had been broken and they doubted, correctly, whether all the towns and fortresses would surrender. They still insisted that, as surety for completion of all the terms of the Treaty, they must have six hostages, and they were adamant that Talbot must be one of them. Their reasons were fairly obvious. He was now, with York, probably alone in being able to raise opposition to France: they considered that his removal from the scene would be generally acknowledged as the indication of England's final collapse, and thus remove all danger of a renewal of the war.

The delegates expressed anger and horror at this proposal. They pointed out that Talbot was now an old man, too old to organise the resistance which they feared, and popular enough in England for very many people to be revolted that the French should insist on holding him prisoner. They added that the unpopularity of Suffolk, Somerset and the Queen would be further increased. The delegation refused to accept the condition and the negotiations were again broken off.

Talbot himself had from the start refused to take any part in the proceedings. Predictably, most of his captains were opposed to allowing him to become a hostage, but Somerset and his friends were in favour of it. After argument had gone on for ten days Somerset had his way and on October 29th, the following hostages were nominated: Lord Shrewsbury (Talbot), Sir John Butler (Ormond's son), Lord Abergavenny, Lord Fauconberg, Thomas, the son of Lord de Roos and thus a grandson of the Duchess of Somerset by her first marriage, and Richard, the son of Sir Thomas Gower. The hostages were told that they would be set free on full completion of the terms of the Treaty, but that they would have to give an undertaking not to bear arms against the French again.

Somerset and the rest of the garrison left immediately under escort for Caen, and thence proceeded to England. Talbot and his fellow hostages were left in a city where, miraculously, bunting carrying the emblem of the lily was already appearing in streets full of people dancing and singing in their happiness. Talbot received a summons almost immediately to attend King Charles at his headquarters in the Monastery of Saint Catherine, together with the other hostages. Neither the King, nor the King of Sicily, nor Dunois, nor Xantrailles, all of whom were present, showed any sign of the triumph which they must have been feeling. On the contrary the King, who had been seated, rose to greet Shrewsbury. He took him by the hand and, raising him up as he bent the knee, said happily: "Talbot, welcome to my court. We are happy to have you here and we hope you will be happy among us."[5]

"Your pardon, Sire," replied Shrewbury stiffly, "I was not at all consulted in this matter."

The King went on: "I pray you to accept this present which we give you as an earnest of our regard for you." From behind him a page brought a cap and a long fur-lined robe in magenta velvet, magenta being the colour of the Talbot livery. The King added: "We hope that you will see fit to wear it on an occasion in the near future." The hostages were then conducted back to their quarters, a man called Sir John D'Aulon and some twenty soldiers being assigned to guard Talbot and to accompany him wherever he went.

King Charles made his State entry into Rouen on 10th

November, 1449 and Talbot was told that his presence was required. It was only six years since Rouen had witnessed a scene of similar magnificence. On that occasion King Charles had brought the young Princess Margaret into the city to hand her over as a bride. Then, Talbot had been one of the leading actors in the pageantry. Now there was much the same pageantry, but his part in it was tragically different. In deference to the King he wore the magenta robe as he and the other hostages were conducted to their places on the chief stand, outside the Archbishop's palace. Shrewsbury was placed next to the Countess of Dunois, and not far from the Chronicler, Waurin, who faithfully recorded every detail of this impressive display of French strength. Waurin, himself an experienced professional soldier, also gives the opinion that the French army now had an excellent organisation, good discipline, regular pay and was the best equipped army in Europe. [6]

The procession was led into the city by squadron after squadron of the corps of archers, now the equal of any which England could produce. Then came retainers, followed by their appropriate French Generals, each under his own banner, and escorted by his liveried esquires. After them came the principal Captains of Towns and the Crown Officers, with the Chancellor of France at their head in full ceremonial dress. There was a pause and then a girl rode into the square, richly dressed and carrying a white banner emblazoned with a large gold fleur-de-lis. After her walked Charles VII, on foot under a panoply, dressed very simply but enveloped in a blue cloak embroidered also with gold fleur-de-lis.

On every side and at every window were smiling faces and crowds of children shouting "Noel" at the top of their voices. Arrived at the Square of Notre Dame, the King kissed the holy relics and the procession disappeared into the Cathedral for a service of thanksgiving. The crowd burst into the streets and, amid the general rejoicing, the hostages were firmly but politely led out of the city. There, horses and an escort were awaiting them, and they were taken to the Castle of Dreux to begin their captivity under the care of Sir John d'Aulon.

Such is the narrative given by Waurin; Monstrelet's has considerable divergencies but, by that date, the reliability of his *Chronicles* of this period is questionable. The following

"Dons et recompensions" quoted in the *Chronicles* of Mathieu d'Escouchy[7] seem to indicate that Talbot and his fellow hostages were held prisoner for a month in Rouen before being taken to Dreux:

"To the said Sir John d'Aulon the sum of 110 Livres Tournois 'a lui baillés comptant' by order of the King, and a further 60 Livres Tournois besides and over and above that 100 Livres Tournais against his expenses in guarding the Palace of Rouen in which Lord Talbot is our prisoner, and for conducting the said Lord Talbot from Rouen to Dreux where the said prisoner is held. And 50 Livres Tournois for distribution to twenty brothers-in-arms who were and are responsible to the said d'Aulon for the security of the said Lord Talbot for expenses while they carried out their duties.

110 Livres Tournoise

"To William Paignon and Hellion de Védille, men-at-arms, the sum of 30 Livres Tournois, to each of them 15 Livres Tournois to each ordered by the King as pay for one month ending 15th December in the Palace of Rouen as guard to Lord Talbot, prisoner and, as part of the company of Sir John d'Aulon at Dreux, to lead and conduct thither the said Lord Talbot, by order of the King.

30 Livres Tournois

"To Benoist le Caron, living at Rouen, the sum of £11.12s.6d, or 7 Escuz and 11/7d, payment ordered by the King for the hire of eleven horses to take Lord Talbot from Rouen to Dreux and other English who are held hostage in that town and for the payment of three men to bring back the horses to Rouen.

£11.12s.6d.

Many towns and fortresses in Western Normandy fell to the French that winter: Valognes, Vire, Bayeux, Caen, Honfleur and even Harfleur, but the towns in the Pay de Caux stubbornly held out, including Falaise. The latter, of which Talbot was Captain and which he regarded almost as his own town, was particularly well defended by Andrew Trobot and Thomas Ethon who were besieged by Dunois himself, supported by artillery under Bureau.[8] During the preceding years Talbot had rebuilt its Keep (which is still known as "Talbot's Tower" today) and the Chapel of St. Prix.[9] The resistance of these towns and the failure of Somerset to fulfil the terms of the Treaty of Rouen meant, of course, that the hostages continued to be held prisoner. But Falaise was a key fortress, and Trobot and Ethon considered that they could, with benefit to all concerned, strike a bargain with Dunois that they would surrender Falaise in exchange for the release of Talbot. Trobot and Ethon sent word to Talbot himself, seeking his approval, and he agreed provided that the English in Falaise would all be allowed to return to England. The offer was referred to King Charles, who refused to consider it on the cryptic grounds that "because of Lord Shrewsbury's upright-ness it would be unworthy of him to give him his freedom on such grounds, and because of his military prowess it would be unwise to give him freedom to use it". [10]

Meanwhile conditions continued to deteriorate in England. The loss of Maine and Anjou, followed so closely by the loss of Normandy, had much the same impact on the people as if part of Kent had been detached from England. York was still serving in Ireland but many powerful figures were coming to his support at home: he had support, too, in the House of Commons, where the lawlessness was attributed to men like Suffolk and Somerset. Justice was being perverted, and ruffians and toughs were being recruited to form private armies. Open warfare existed between the retainers of families such as the Courtenays and the Bouvilles in Devon, or even between Archbishop Kemp and Sir William Plumpton in Yorkshire. In February 1449 Parliament set up a Commission "to inquire into the incidence and causes of murders and riots against the peace" and to ensure that "liveries be certified by every Sheriff". This amounted to a census of liveried retainers but it had little effect.

Parliament met again in November and feeling ran high against Suffolk both on account of the disasters in France, where Rouen was on the point of capitulation, and the anarchy at home. Suffolk and a man named Tailboys, an upstart who a year or two later managed to bully his way back into the Queen's favour, were accused of plotting the murder of Lord Cromwell and Lord Moleyns. The Lords refused to indict Suffolk on what they said was inadequate evidence but, in February 1450, the Commons moved a formal indictment on eight counts. The chief of these was that he had plotted with the French an invasion of England and had incited them to renew the war in France, as a result of which Lord

Fauconberg and Lord Shrewsbury had been taken prisoner. Queen Margaret did all she could to postpone or evade the proceedings; but additional charges were brought, including one of embezzlement. Suffolk and his friends fought hard. He himself was successful in the Lords, who again refused to prosecute him; but Tailboys, a Member of Parliament for Lincolnshire, failed to carry the Commons. They made him pay £3,000 damages for the attack on Cromwell, and they insisted that Suffolk must be banished.

The King and Queen had to admit defeat and the order for banishment was signed on May 1st. Suffolk had sailed from Ipswich the previous day, but that did not save him. His headless body was found on the beach at Dover on May 2nd. This was the signal for further violence. The Bishop of Salisbury, a friend of Suffolk's, was dragged from the Altar in Edington Church in Wiltshire, and murdered on the top of the nearby Downs. (It was he who had married Henry and Margaret.) At the same time a man called Jack Cade insti-gated a rebellion in Kent. He had the support of the yeomen farmers and his attack was aimed at corrupt officials. King Henry showed, for once, considerable courage and initiative in dealing with it, but risings took place elsewhere. The threat to law and order was sufficient to bring York back from Ireland with a force of 4,000 men. Somerset protested against this and Queen Margaret sided with him. York and Somerset, the representatives of the two great Houses of York and Lancaster, were now openly challenging each other for power. On a day in July they actually confronted each other in the Temple gardens, and there the Red Rose challenged the White. The threat of civil war was nearer than ever.

That same month, on July 10th, 1450, agreement was reached in France for Talbot's release in exchange for the surrender of Falaise. The Treaty is a long and very detailed document. It gave to the people of Falaise, both French and English, complete liberty to stay or to leave the town, with an amnesty for everyone. The town was free to make a break with the past and to start afresh under the French King's jurisdic-tion. In return Shrewsbury promised, under Article 4, as follows: [11]

"And for the doing of the things aforesaid the King is content to deliver the person of my said Lord, the Earl of

Shrewsbury, free and quit so far as he can be concerned of everything in which he can be held and bound in consequence of the Agreement lately made in the City of Rouen provided that he will promise that he will go to Rome before he will return into the Country of England, as he himself has given the King to understand that it is his wish, devotion and intention so to do . . ." In accordance with the Rouen agreement Talbot also undertook never to bear arms against the French again. In view of his great age this then seemed an easy promise to give.

Charles himself had assumed command of the long siege of Falaise, and on July 11th, 1450, when it was lifted, Talbot could at last set out on his pilgrimage to Rome.[12] There he was received by Pope Nicholas, to whom he presented gold and silver plate, and some horses which King Charles had sent by his hand. The Pope took great interest in all that Talbot had to tell him of affairs in England and France. He announced that he would send the French Cardinal, d'Estouteville, to King Charles, and the Bishop of Ravenna to King Henry, to urge upon both of them that they should make peace with each other. They returned before Talbot left Rome and reported that King Charles paid lip service to the cause of peace, but that King Henry (presumably Somerset speaking for him) declared that England would not make peace so long as France held parts of English territory which she had conquered.

Talbot arrived back in England in the early months of 1451. The country was still stunned from the violent events of the previous year. Jack Cade's insurgents had actually invaded London and had murdered those who tried to stop them. Talbot's old friend, Sir Matthew Gough, who had led him to the relief of Le Mans as long ago as 1428, and who had only recently returned to England after being ransomed following his capture at Formigny, when his horse had foundered beneath him, now died trying to prevent the mob from crossing London Bridge. The rebels had even succeeded in opening the gaols of King's Bench and Marshalsea, and in holding the City Aldermen to ransom. The rebellion had petered out eventually, but the country had experienced widespread violence for the first time since Bolingbroke had seized the throne. There was indeed a similarity between

England in those last months of King Richard's reign and the winter of 1451.

In retirement at last, the Shrewsburys built themselves a hunting lodge at Sheepscombe, near Painswick, part of which still survives under the name of "Lodge Farm". The long-standing quarrel between the Talbots and the Berkeleys flared up again, because a County Jury had found that James, 11th Lord Berkeley, was his uncle's heir rather than Margaret Shrewsbury. Her eldest son, John Lisle, was now married to Joan Cheddar, and they had a son, Thomas. John Lisle entered into the feud with enthusiasm. When Berkeley's men plundered Painswick, he retaliated. Soon afterwards another Berkeley raiding party assaulted one of the Talbot stewards, who had just returned from collecting rents. They threatened the poor man with terrible torture from a red-hot iron bar unless he handed over the money. He did so, but when the raiding party returned to their horses, they found themselves surrounded by Talbot men under John Lisle. He fastened them to their horses and the whole party rode back to Berkeley Castle. Dawn was breaking as they arrived, but it was still too dark to identify badges. The leader of the Berkeley men, with John Lisle's dagger at his back, hailed the watch. There was a pause while the yeoman was sent to ask for the keys. The drawbridge was lowered and the portcullis raised. In rushed John Lisle and his men, who captured Berkeley and his four sons, and carried them off prisoners to Goodrich. The Talbots seized Berkeley Castle and held it for some years.

In February 1452, York and his son, the Earl of March, raised an army said to number some 10,000 men and moved through Gloucestershire towards London. The King and Somerset took the field against them, but, by a miracle of restraint on all sides, peace prevailed. York took himself off to Wigmore Castle, after being assured by the King that he would place Somerset under arrest.

Such was the state of affairs when Talbot received a summons to attend the King at Westminster with all speed. It is not difficult to imagine with what reluctance the old man dragged himself out of the peaceful beauty of the Painswick valley, after his brief months of retirement there, and set off for London. Fear and tension was evident in the villages through which they rode, but as they passed through Oxford the building of the New College was continuing apace. Nearer London, on the banks of the Thames, the buildings of the school at Eton were rising in the shadow of the walls of Windsor Castle. England had sunk to a low level politically, but her craftsmen were hard at work.

Talbot presented himself at Westminster at the end of March, 1452.

CHAPTER XIV

DURING THE SUMMER OF 1450, when it had become clear to King Charles that all serious opposition to him in northern France was at an end, he had turned his attention to Gascony. The position there was very different from that in the north, in that the native population was strongly pro-English and had been so for nearly three centuries. This was not entirely disinterested: the wine merchants of Gascony shipped four million gallons of their produce to England annually.[1] While Charles regarded it as a province of France, its inhabitants regarded him as a foreign conquering power, and, as the attack led by the ubiquitous Dunois developed, the Gascons had appealed to Henry VI for help. None had been forthcoming; there were very few English troops in the area, and the Gascons themselves had no army. The Mayor of Bordeaux had put up a fight, but suffered a crushing defeat by Count D'Orval in the Mèdoc. In the spring of 1451 Charles increased the weight of his attack by sending Jean Bureau south with artillery. On June 2nd, the French captured Fronsac, a key fortress which had always been garrisoned by English-born soldiers.[2] Bordeaux had reluctantly surrendered on June 23rd, and a week later Dunois staged a ceremonial entry into the city which was even more impressive in scale and grandeur than Charles' own entry into Rouen seven months previously.[3] Over 10,000 men took part, and most of the French leaders of both Church and State were present.

Dunois himself represented King Charles, and was received by the City Council, which included Lords de Lesparre and de Monteferrant. The Archbishop conducted a service in the Cathedral, in the course of which Sir Olivier de Cotiny, the newly appointed Seneschal of Gascony, led the City Council and a large body of local nobles in declaring before God their allegiance to the French King.[4]

Bayonne surrendered on 21st August, and the whole ceremony was repeated there. Waurin comments: "And thus, by the Grace of God, was all France conquered for the French except Calais". But trouble soon threatened Charles in the far north, where an insurrection took place in Ghent, sparked off by the salt tax. Confident that the whole of France now owed allegiance to him, Charles withdrew his forces to Flanders.

But he had under-estimated the determination of the Gascons. A mere three months after the elaborate ceremonial in Bordeaux several burghers, led by de Lesparre and de Montferrant, escaped in disguise. Their object was to make a last passionate appeal to Henry VI to liberate them from the French. But the spark which had inspired Henry to take action against the Duke of York had been short-lived, and he had sunk back into his usual lethargy leaving the reins of government in the hands of Margaret and Somerset. They had trouble enough on their hands in England, and the arrival of the deputation from Bordeaux was an extra and, on the face of it, rather unnecessary problem with which to grapple.

To both of them, for very different reasons, Talbot was the obvious person to relieve them of this burden. To the Queen, he was a dear friend and an entirely reliable counsellor. To Somerset, on the other hand, Talbot was still a possible figure round whom the opposition could rally. He was too old to initiate such a movement, but his age now gave him the status of an elder statesman. To send him in pursuit of a hopeless cause in far-away Gascony, whence he would probably never return, would dispose of one of the dangers to Somerset's power. Moreover Gascony's appeal was one which a man of Talbot's character was most unlikely to resist.

Talbot's own reaction is not known; but his Will, (vide Appendix B) which he executed the day before he sailed for Bordeaux, gives some indication of his thoughts. He was under no illusion that he would return alive; he was also a little bitter "considering the great cost and injury" to his person "occasioned by (his) said Sovereign Lord". That clause can only be read as referring to King Henry VI. Talbot can hardly be blamed for such feelings. All French historians assert that he was then 80 years old, though the indications are that he was nearer 70, in an age when few men lived to reach the age of 50. During all those years he had had practically no respite from service. Another indication given by his Will is that of family tensions. His family by his first wife is never mentioned, except for the one brief clause leaving only the essentially "Talbot" Lordships of Goodrich and Irchenfield to his eldest son, from whom it would seem he became estranged after

Maud's death. Colour is lent to this possibility by his son's marriage to Elizabeth, daughter of Lord Ormond. In the long dispute between his father and his father-in-law, it must have been difficult for the young man to decide which of the two he should support, and he may well have sympathised with Ormond. The fact remains that, in the concluding paragraph of his Will, Talbot specifically requires his son not to intercept or to hinder the performance of it and adds, somewhat drastically perhaps, that, if that were to occur, the Executors were to sell the lands rather than allow his son and heir to succeed to them.

Further indication of discord between the two halves of John Talbot's family may be seen in the marriage, in 1453, of Joan, his youngest daughter by Maud, to James, Lord Berkeley. The Berkeley-Warwick dispute was then at its height and Joan's action can be seen as a calculated blow to a step-mother for whom she had little affection. The marriage certainly did nothing to reconcile the two families and the lawsuit between them was not finally settled until 1609.

With regard to Talbot's undertaking not to bear arms again against the French King, and its bearing on his task, he absolved himself on the grounds that he had been invited by the Bordelais, not to make war against the French, but to rule them: he would act solely from an administrative head-quarters. He extracted from Somerset the promise of pay for an immediate muster of 3,000 men, to be followed by a further reinforcement in the spring of 1453. He sailed with 24 ships from Portsmouth on 2nd September, 1452, and the sun was rising on 17th October as he led his small fleet up the wide waters of the Gironde Estuary. The flat coasts in the distance on either side might be either hostile or friendly. It was true that Lord Lesparre and the rest of the Bordeaux deputation had assured him that the whole of Gascony would welcome him, but they had strongly vested interests in persuading the English to return to their Province. King Charles had imposed crippling taxes on their wine exports when he took over the country, and trade had virtually ceased. It was this, and the hurt done to the natural pride of the Gascons, that had forced honourable men into betraying the oaths of allegiance which they had so recently given. The critical question so far as Talbot was concerned, was whether the populace regarded these men as traitors or as patriotic freedom-fighters. He based his operational plan on the assumption that he would be landing on a hostile shore.

Accordingly, instead of sailing on up the Estuary to Bordeaux, he landed at Grayon, a small seaport on Lord Lesparre's estate, and disposed his little army in a defensive position while stores, horses and equipment were brought ashore. He established his headquarters at a house eight miles inland. It is still called 'Château Talbot' and commemorates the origin of its name on the labels of its wine bottles.

Talbot's doubts about his reception were resolved the very next day when the citizens of Bordeaux rose against the French authorities and threw them out of the city. The news was brought to him by Sir Bertelot de Rivière and Sir Loys de Bretail, who greeted Talbot as their deliverer and insisted on addressing him as "Le Roi Talbot". They brought with them, as evidence of their success, the erstwhile Seneschal, Sir Olivier de Cotiny, who had been captured trying to escape from the City. He had been one of King Charles' commanders during the ignominious marching and counter-marching which attended the siege of Pontoise, and no doubt had a considerable respect for Talbot as a result of that experience.

The official entry of the English Viceroy into Bordeaux was arranged to take place five days later, on October 23rd. Sir Bertelot and his companions were disappointed at the small size of the English army, and it certainly compared badly with the great strength so recently demonstrated by the French: it seemed a mere handful of men to those Bordelais who had watched the procession of ten thousand led by Dunois only eighteen months previously. But, if colourful grandeur had been the keynote of that French procession, plain business-like simplicity was that of the English re-entry.

Preceded only by his old Herald, now white-haired and in somewhat faded livery, but still an impressive figure, and attended by two esquires, Talbot led his men in through the West Gate. Bound as he was by his oath not to bear arms against the French, he was mounted, not on a charger, but on a small grey cob. Against its flanks the long sweep of the magenta surcoat given to him by King Charles showed up in sharp contrast. In spite of his great age, he still rode erect and firm, and the only visible sign of his years was the white hair

falling below his velvet cap. Here indeed was the soldier who
had terrorised the French for years, but with a moving
simplicity which won the hearts of the ordinary people of
Bordeaux. The little procession moved into the square in front
of the Cathedral and drew up before its doors. Talbot's Herald
advanced and, in a resounding voice, read out the Letters
Patent of Talbot's appointment. The long rolling Latin
phrases echoed round the square, referring to "Our very dear
Cousin, Johannem Comitem Salopiae" and going on to give
him full powers as our "locum tenentem in our Dukedom of
Aquitaine", for a term of six years. He was empowered to
contract, to rule, and to make appointments and dismissals as
he considered fit. The document was dated "per ipsum Regem
et Concilium" at Westminster, the second day of September,
1452.[5]

As the Herald finished reading, Sir Henry de Pays, the
Mayor, with a number of the chief burghers, knelt before
Talbot presenting him with the keys of the city and declaring
their allegiance to King Henry VI of England. The
Archbishop conducted a short service of thanksgiving, and the
ceremony was over. That night messengers were sent speeding
throughout Aquitaine with the news that "Le Roi Talbot" had
liberated Bordeaux.

It took Talbot a fortnight to deal with the local administrative problems, and it was only then that he could turn his
attention to the wider issue of controlling the whole Province.
To do so he needed to consult with, and obtain information
from, the late Seneschal.[6] But Sir Olivier de Cotiny was the
prisoner of Sir Bertelot de Rivière and, as the possession of
prisoners included the right to their ransom money, it was a
right which was jealously guarded; particularly where a
valuable prisoner such as the Seneschal was concerned. It was
therefore with considerable reluctance that Sir Bertelot agreed
that Sir Olivier should be interrogated by Talbot. The two
men knew each other's position well enough to be extremely
frank. Sir Olivier knew that Talbot's resources were slender,
and that he was most unlikely to receive much in the way of
reinforcements from England. Talbot knew that, if Sir Olivier
collaborated with him, he would be branded a traitor but
that, in any case, having lost Bordeaux, he had no future in
France. After a first formal interview Sir Olivier was sent back

to his captors to consider his position. Five days later Talbot
sent for him again. [7] An agreement was reached, presumably
with Sir Bertelot's consent, that Sir Olivier would collaborate
in return for a safe conduct to England. Even if he had
anticipated his captivity at Goodrich until 1457 he would, at
that time, probably have chosen it rather than either of the
alternatives.

Talbot learned that the French had withdrawn most of their
troops northwards to deal with the trouble in Ghent, and that
an early attack in any strength was very unlikely. Lord d'Orval
was in Touraine with about six hundred men, and this was the
most likely direction from which a counter-attack would
come. Only a few of the French garrisons were at a strength
which would allow them to put up anything of a fight: the
most determined resistance was likely to come from the town
of Fronsac which, like the English, the French regarded as
"the strongest fortress in all that country and the very key to
Guienne". [8] It was commanded by one of King Charles' most
able Captains, Joachim Rohault. Of the remainder,
Clerment, Bayonne, and Périgeux were the most likely to hold
out, but the western part of the Province would give its
allegiance to Talbot at the least threat of force. Chalais,
Libourne, Saint Emilion, Castillon, among other towns, had
already sent in deputations declaring their allegiance, and
Talbot decided that he would reinforce those garrisons to
provide a bulwark against the north while he himself carried
out a *démarche* to the south. In the meantime he dispatched
Sir Olivier de Cotiny to England in his, Talbot's, own vessel
the *Margaret*, under escort of Sir William Lucy.

During the weeks which followed, Talbot consolidated his
position in Aquitaine in spite of Lord d'Orval's attack, which
was launched, as expected, against Chalais, Périgeux and
Castillon. The garrisons held it off, and Lord d'Orval retired
to the north. Talbot himself marched south on Bayonne,
which capitulated after a brief show of resistance, and he then
returned north by way of Saint Severs, Aiguillon and
Bergerac. He had formally appointed his grandson Thomas,
to be Governor of Bordeaux. It is curious to note that, in spite
of the wide powers given to him, the instrument appointing
Thomas took the form of a declaration in French, sealed by
"John Earl of Shrewsbury" and dated 13th November, 1452,

but nevertheless requiring ratification in Latin by the King at Westminster on 17th January, 1453. [9] Although he was not himself involved in any fighting, and acted only as the administrative head of the campaign, it involved long marches, followed by arduous hours spent dealing with a constant stream of petitions and complaints. It was thus a considerable feat of endurance for a man of his age. Nevertheless, by the spring of 1453 Talbot had established complete control from the River Garonne southwards to the Pyrenees. A minor aggravation at this time was that his digestion had become very bad. This was not altogether surprising, as he now had only one tooth left in his upper jaw. It was a wisdom tooth which hurt him so much that he told his Herald that he was going to have it out as he would be better off without it.

It was in March that the first information reached Talbot that the French King had started to collect an army for a southern campaign. The informant went on to say, jokingly, that it seemed that there would be more cannons than men in this army as the King had given Jean and Jasper Bureau a free hand to have as many made as they thought fit.

It was in March too that the additional troops which had been promised by Somerset in his original conversation with Talbot, arrived in France. They numbered some six thousand men and included a contingent under John Lisle. He had been indentured to supply two bannerettes, four knights, and eight hundred archers on foot. [10] It held him to "do us service of war for a quarter of a year in our Duchy of Guyenne for the surety and safeguard of the same", and it set out the precise terms of his engagement, including the fact that he was to be paid at the rate of six shillings a day from the date on which he sailed from Plymouth. It was fifty-six years since his father had received a similar indenture for service to King Richard II in Ireland.

In April, 1453, the form of attack which the French were planning was beginning to become apparent. No less than three armies were converging very slowly on Bordeaux: one from the south-east, a second from the east, and a third from the north-east. King Charles himself was mustering a reserve at Tours. Their united strength would be overwhelming; but if Talbot could engage them individually, the strength of his Anglo-Gascon force would be almost their equal. Yet if he advanced too far to meet, say, the north-east threat (which was the most serious one), his right flank would be open to attack from one of the other advancing armies. His strategy would have to be a matter of exact timing, and it would inevitably mean that certain towns fell to the French advance before he could halt it.

Talbot sent his senior commanders out around the Province to encourage the Gascons, and to explain his strategy to them, but there were not lacking those who said that he was now too old. Where, they asked, was the fiery dash for which the "English Achilles" was renowned? He should be striking at the French before they came too close instead of sitting in his headquarters at Bordeaux. This murmuring increased when, at the end of June, the French column under Jean Bureau captured Chalais and beheaded all its defenders as traitors.

By July 10th that same column was approaching Castillon, a matter of thirty miles from Bordeaux. It was clear that, after capturing Castillon, Bureau would move on to Libourne, which was ten miles closer to the capital and within striking distance of it. There he would not only be within range of a surprise counter-attack, but, pinned against the River Dordogne, it would be possible for Talbot to destroy him; and destruction rather than mere defeat was an essential element of Talbot's strategy.

On July 13th, a deputation waited on Talbot at his headquarters in Bordeaux. It was led by the Mayor of Castillon, but also contained several of the leading citizens of Bordeaux.

"Sire," the Mayor said, "as you know the French are at our gates. They number some seven thousand men, they have three hundred cannons, and Castillon cannot withstand their attack. Yet you make no move to help us. Are we to suffer the same fate as Chalais?"[11]

Talbot patiently explained to them that Castillon was too far away for him to make a lightning strike which would take the French by surprise without risk of his being caught by the army advancing from the Upper Dordogne. There were murmurs of anger and dismay.[12] "We asked the English King to free us from the French," they said. "When you arrived we helped you to throw them out. Are we now to be sacrificed to them just because thirty miles is too far for an old man to ride?" A voice was even heard to say: "The old man has lost his courage: he should be replaced by a younger one."

Yet again Talbot explained that to save Castillon might imperil Bordeaux, and even the whole of Gascony; but they remained convinced that he could save Castillon had he the energy and the courage to do so. That allegation was a bitter one for the gallant old man to accept, but a more serious matter was that unless he could win a quick and startling victory over the French very soon, the towns of Gascony would begin to go over to the enemy in self-defence. With many misgivings, and against his better judgment, Talbot decided to attack Bureau at Castillon.

First he sent scouts up the valley of the Dordogne and along the line to locate enemy outposts. By July 15th he had received their reports and made his plan, and he called a Conference of his Commanders. Bordeaux was full of spies, very ready to sell information to the French, and it was important that the plans should be kept secret even from the troops until after they had left Bordeaux. They would deliver a surprise attack at Castillon and, because of the falling off of confidence in his personal leadership, he would personally command the operation although still bound by his oath not to wear armour. The French had outposts on the Libourne to Castillon Road, and a thousand archers in the Priory of Saint Lorent just north of the town; there were also a thousand Bretons in the woods some two miles to the north-east of Castillon who, if all went well, could be prevented from interfering with the main attack. Jean Bureau had placed his encampment on the far side of Castillon from Bordeaux, which could only mean that he wished to keep his line of retreat open and not be caught between Castillon and any relieving army. He had also placed it inside the "U" which is formed by the junction of the little stream, the Lidoire, with the Dordogne, about five hundred yards east of Castillon.

The Lidoire was narrow, but with such steep sides as to be an obstacle to horses. The Dordogne, on the other hand, was about four hundred yards wide, and, even in July when the water was low, the current would be strong and the ford, somewhere opposite the French encampment, difficult to locate. The distance from the bank of the Dordogne to the encampment would be about six hundred yards over flat and open ground.

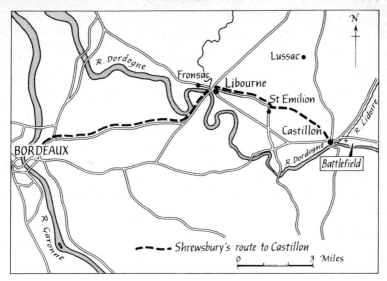

Talbot's route from Bordeaux to Castillon

Talbot proposed to march at the noon the next day, July 16th, to Libourne, and he reckoned that Bureau would at once hear that he had done so and would expect him to move on up the valley next day. This surmise would be endorsed when Bureau learned that the English force had fed and made camp on arrival at Libourne. By then they would have marched twenty miles and, as the weather was stiflingly hot they would need to rest. But at dusk, (about 10.0 p.m. at that time of the year), the march would be resumed, not along the road to Castillon, but up into the woods to the north. There, there would only be rough tracks, but Talbot had arranged reliable guides who would bring them down into the valley from the north. The timing would be so arranged that his mounted archers and men-at-arms would arrive at their destination at dawn.

In this way the French archers in the Priory would be taken by surprise, and Talbot detailed Sir Thomas Evringham to take charge of that attack. After capturing the Priory they would await the arrival of the main body before launching the attack on Bureau's encampment. This pause would provide a much needed interval during which men and horses could feed and recover from the gruelling night march. When the main body arrived it would move straight into the attack across the Lidoire, while the advance guard would cross the stream by the ford near its junction with the Dordogne and attack Bureau from the direction of the river: this would take them over the open ground ideal for mounted men and Bureau would thus find himself being attacked from both front and rear.

John Lisle pointed out to his father that a march of over thirty miles followed by a battle was too much for a man of Talbot's age and that, as his oath prevented him from doing any actual fighting, he should allow Moleyns or another to take charge of the operation; but Talbot would have none of it.

CHAPTER XV

TALBOT MARCHED OUT of Bordeaux at noon the next day, July 16th. [1] Behind him came five hundred men-at-arms and eight hundred mounted archers. They were followed by three thousand two hundred men on foot. It was a small force with which to attack a prepared encampment that was known to be defended by some seven thousand men, excluding the archers in the Priory and the Bretons to the north east. Talbot could count on no help at all from his artillery, which would be left far behind on the march. The odds against him were frighteningly long, but he had come to regard that as inevitable and it did not deter him.

After the gruelling march to Libourne the English troops thankfully threw themselves down to rest, but at 10.0 o'clock they were quietly roused by their commanders. They marched out of camp and disappeared into the woods to the north of Libourne. It was not until the first halt, an hour after they had started, that each Commander explained the plan of attack to his men, and now the march took on a new character. As far as Libourne it had been merely an oppressively hot route march. Now it became yet another of those night approach marches for which Talbot had become famous. The men talked in hushed voices, and the mounted contingent increased their speed by alternating half an hour's walk with half an hour's trot. They thus gradually drew ahead of those on foot.

At length the trees gave way to vines and then, out of the darkness and seeming to loom right over their heads, a large building was outlined on their right. Dogs barked and lights appeared in one or two of the windows. The guide muttered that it was the Bishop's Palace at St. Emilion. The track was climbing more gently now, as it followed the edge of the ridge, and down to their right they could see occasional lights and even an occasional silver gleam where the waters of the Dordogne reflected the stars. Ahead of them the sky began to pale with the first hint of dawn as they swung right-handed down the hillside. Now they could see the faint outlines of Castillon's turreted walls. The guide had brought them out at

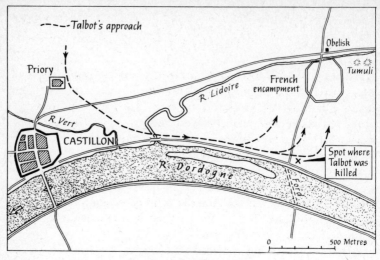

----- Talbot's approach

Priory

Obelisk

Tumuli

French
encampment

R. Lidoire

R. Vert

CASTILLON

R. Dordogne

Ford

Spot where
Talbot was
killed

×

0   500 Metres

Battle of Castillon, 1453

exactly the right spot and at the right moment. Silently he
pointed to a building faintly visible three hundred yards away.
"There is the Priory", he said.

Evringham needed no more orders and a few moments later
the silence was broken by shouts and screams of the French
archers. Many of them were slaughtered in their beds, but
many succeeded in escaping in the dim light. They could be
heard, pursuers and pursued, making for the French encampment a mile away. From there, too, a clamour arose as the
French army stood hurriedly to its weapons. Among Talbot's
men the completeness of the surprise, and the ease with which
the Priory had been taken, raised everybody's spirits. It would
be two hours before the main body caught up with them and,
by then, all would be ready for the second phase of the
operation. Talbot posted outposts and ordered his men to feed
and water their horses and then to have a meal themselves.

The French encampment was screened from the Priory by
trees and a fold in the ground, so Talbot sent Evringham
forward to reconnoitre. He himself climbed stiffly off his horse
and went into the Priory, which was found to be well stocked
with food and wine. He ordered his Chaplain to prepare Mass,
after which he would have a meal.

While the Chaplain was busy in the Chapel, Talbot went

round among the men. They were in the highest spirits and
looking forward to the coming encounter with the French.
Some of them showed him rough banners which they had
made bearing very rude remarks about the French King and
his right to occupy the throne of France. [2] He was still with
the men when excited voices were heard approaching. One of
the outposts was bringing in a man whom Talbot recognised
as one of the Burghers of Castillon who had accused him of
being too old and timorous. Breathlessly the man gasped out
that, from the town walls, he had seen the French running
away. He had seen the dust cloud raised by their horses'
hooves: unless Talbot attacked at once they would all escape.

Talbot moved aside. His men were tired and had not
finished their meal. The main body would still be four miles
away; but perhaps he should risk attacking without them.
Enemy flight at his surprise attack was nothing new. At that
moment Evringham returned and reported that he had seen
no signs of flight. [3] He agreed that, from where he had stood,
he had been unable to see the far side of the encampment, but
what he had seen was a very strong position with a great many
cannon. He advised Talbot to wait for the main body to arrive
before launching his attack. Talbot's dilemma was whether he
should wait and risk losing contact with the enemy, with all
that this would mean for the future of his strategy, or whether
he should risk a pitched battle against a strong position with
odds of about six to one against him. At that moment his
Chaplain appeared to say that all was ready for Mass. In
sudden decision Talbot waved him aside. "I will hear Mass
when I have defeated the enemy," he said, and he ordered the
trumpeter to sound the advance. He called for his horse and,
moments later, led his little force at a gallop down the gentle
slope to the Dordogne at the point where the Lidoire joins it:
Then over the shallow ford and up the sunken track along the
river bank for five hundred yards, followed by a left wheel up
and out onto the plain at the far side of which was the French
position.

During the past four days Bureau, who must have been
confident that Talbot would come out to attack him, had
worked feverishly on the defences of his encampment. (Its
outline can still be discerned.) It was an irregular shaped oval,
backed on the north side by the steep banks of the Lidoire and

surrounded, over the rest of its perimeter, by a deep ditch backed by a palisaded rampart. The muzzles of no fewer than three hundred cannon projected over this rampart; there were so many that they had to be placed wheel to wheel to get them all into position. The crews now stood ready behind them with their lighted fuses flaring in the early morning sun.

This was the unnerving sight which met Talbot's eyes as he came into view. He had been given misleading information by the Burgher. The French were not in retreat: they had merely sent their horses to the rear to make room inside the encampment for those archers who had escaped from the Priory. Talbot hesitated, but only for a moment. Confident in the fighting qualities of his men, he deployed them along the river bank and made everyone dismount. He alone remained mounted and the conspicuous sight of this solitary horseman, on a grey cob and wearing no armour, was one that nobody who took part in the battle would ever forget.

He gave the signal for the assault and, with the battle cry "Talbot! Saint George!" the Anglo-Gascons advanced and engaged. The French gunners stood behind their cannons waiting for the order to apply their fuses, while the solid phalanx of men-at-arms advanced across the grass towards them. At a range of two hundred yards Bureau gave the order to fire and the whole palisade erupted in smoke and flame. As it cleared, gaps could be seen in the ranks of advancing men, but they were quickly closed and the advance continued. They were closer still before the order came to charge the ramparts. The grey cob stood like a rock as the attack streamed past, and Talbot's personal bodyguard gathered round him while he directed and encouraged the attack.

Soon his troops reached the ditch at the foot of the palisade: on the left a cheer went up as Sir Thomas Evringham was seen to plant his banner on the top of it, but he was killed the next instant. Several times the palisade appeared to be taken, only to be recovered by the French in desperate hand-to-hand fighting, as the struggle swayed this way and that, the figure on the grey cob was always there when things seemed to be going badly. He seemed to bear a charmed life amid the hail of cannon balls which fell around him, killing as many as five or six men at one shot.

After an hour Talbot saw the leading units of his main body

crossing the Lidoire on his left. He sent a message over to their
Captain, Lord Kendall, ordering him to attack the French
right flank and to throw in other units piecemeal as they
arrived. Kendall sent a message back saying that he would do
so, but added that he only had with him the advanced
elements, the main body being still some distance away. The
disparity in numbers was so great that Kendall's diversion did
little to relieve the situation; but at least it encouraged the
Anglo-Gascons, who pressed home their own attack even more
vigorously. Again the ramparts were taken, and again the
attackers were flung back. The result still hung in the balance
when Talbot saw movement away to his right. It was the
Bretons, who had now had time to move in from their position
and were about to attack his right flank. He directed Lord
Moleyns to disengage his men from the ramparts to meet this
new threat. Bureau was quick to notice this from his command
post inside the encampment, and seized his opportunity. He
ordered his men to leave the palisade and to sally forth to
attack.

The battle now reached its height. Under the weight of the
combined French and Breton attack the Anglo-Gascon line
began to give way. In spite of all his efforts Talbot could not
stem the movement and, foot by foot, his men were pressed
back towards the river. It was then that Talbot found John
Lisle fighting alongside his hard-pressed bodyguard, and that
he himself, attacked on all sides finally regarded himself as
absolved from his oath and drew his sword. The two men
fought side by side, the younger on foot, the old man on his
grey cob, whose flanks were now steaming in the hot sun.

Then there came a pause in the fighting. The English had
been driven back a full three hundred yards from the encampment and only occasional French cannon balls whistled past or
hit some unlucky target with a sickening thud. Talbot took
advantage of the lull and turned to his son: above the din he
made it clear to John Lisle that, while he himself would try to
hold the enemy back, he wanted his son to take what men he
could and get away across the river behind them.

John Lisle looked up at his father as he sat leaning forward
in his saddle. His velvet cap had long since fallen off and his
white hair blew in the light breeze. His surcoat had got in the
way of his sword arm, and he had flung it away. Blood flowed

from a cut on his jaw, but through the blood and sweat and dirt the young man could see that his father knew the position was hopeless. Indignantly he refused to leave him. Talbot first urged and then ordered his son to make his escape across the ford, telling him that as it was his first campaign no reproach could possibly redound to him.[4] But John Lisle absolutely refused to leave the old man. Instead he raised his voice to a shout, rallying more men around them with the cry "Talbot! St. George!" Soon some thirty men had fought their way to the spot where father and son stood, the grey cob making a good rallying point.

The ground fell away slightly behind them to where, only a bare hundred yards away, the wide waters of the Dordogne swirled past. Across it, and now heading diagonally upstream, there was a straggling line of bobbing heads as some of the more faint-hearted succeeded in locating the ford. The bodies of others who had been unlucky could be seen floating away downstream. At that moment the French onslaught was renewed, and the little band fought back, standing shoulder to shoulder round the grey cob; but at each attack a number of them fell, and then the end came. A chance cannon ball struck the cob's off-side quarter and knocked her off her feet. As she fell she pinned Talbot's left leg under her and he lay helplessly on his left side, half face-downwards on the ground.

John Lisle, and those few who now remained alive, fought desperately to protect the fallen man. One by one they were killed. John Lisle fell to a sword thrust and a moment later a battle axe went crashing into the back of Talbot's skull as he lay on the ground. The grey cob, recovering from the numbing effect of the cannon ball, struggled to her feet and galloped away, riderless, down the banks of the river towards Castillon.

It was the sight of that empty, careering saddle which finally broke the nerve of the remnant of Talbot's small army. They broke and fled. The exultant French pursued them across the river and up into the hills, as far afield as St. Emilion. Soon the only sound on the field of battle were the cries and groans of the wounded and the dying.

But amongst the French there were contradictory accounts as to whether Talbot had been killed or merely wounded.[5] Bureau sent parties to sort out the dead for burial and, above all, to identify the bodies of the Anglo-Gascon commanders. It was important to know for certain whether Talbot was or was not amongst them. But such was the carnage that many individuals were unrecognisable and, as night fell, the search had to be abandoned.

Talbot's old Herald was amongst several who arrived the next morning to enquire for their masters, and he was asked would he know his master if he saw him. Matthieu d'Escouchy continues the narrative: "He replied joyfully, deeming him to be still alive: thereupon he was taken to the place . . . and they said to him 'look and see if that be your master'. Then he changed colour all at once and at first gave no opinion. He knelt down, however, and said he would straightway know the truth: and then he put one of his fingers into the dead man's mouth and felt on the left side for the place of a tooth he knew for certain his master had lost . . . and immediately, still kneeling, he kissed the mouth of the corpse and said: 'Oh my Lord and my master! Oh my Lord and my master! It is indeed you! I pray God to pardon your sins. I have been your officer-at-arms forty years or more: it is time I gave you back your trust.' Making sad cries and lamentations and with tears streaming from his eyes most piteously, he took off his coat of arms and laid it over his master."

POSTSCRIPT

FOUR THOUSAND MEN DIED in the battle of Castillon, which brought to an end the Hundred Years War between France and England. Only a remnant of demoralised English fugitives and prisoners remained overseas. The body of John, Lord Lisle, was never identified.

Following the identification of his master's body by Talbot's Herald the French commanders conferred as to what should be done with it. Both Dunois and Jean Bureau insisted that full military honours should be paid to it. They gave him temporary burial on the spot where he died, and referred the matter to the French King for instructions. With their messenger they sent Talbot's Standard (which had been captured by a Breton named Oliver Griffart), and his gorgerette (the crescent of steel worn as a chest protection). The King expressed satisfaction on seeing this evidence of John's defeat and death, but added sadly: "God have mercy on the good Knight to whom this belonged." Talbot's brigandine (shirt) found its way to the Chateau Royal d'Amboise. [1]

In 1856 a Monsieur Teulet, a member of the French Society of Antiquaries, was shown a sword (he does not say where) which had recently been recovered from the River Dordogne and which bore, in bad Latin, the inscription "Sum Talboti pro vinceri inimicos meos".

There has always been doubt as to what initially happened to Talbot's body, but the following seems the most likely course of events. His heart was carefully embalmed, wrapped in crimson velvet, and taken to Whitchurch where it was buried in the porch (see later). His body was then taken for burial to Falaise, the town of which he had been Captain for so many years.

The French Captains erected a Chapel as a memorial to him at Castillon. It was built on the actual site of his death and was called "Notre Dame de Talbot". It was demolished during the French Revolution, but a cross was subsequently erected on the same spot which is still known as "Le Tombe de Talbot".

In 1493, Gilbert, 3rd Earl of Shrewsbury, a grandson,

The Memorial to John Talbot at Castillon.

This was erected in the nineteenth century on the site of his death.
The Stone Cross in the foreground was probably part of the original
Memorial, a Chapel, built by the French in the fifteenth century
and destroyed during the French Revolution.

The Parish Church at Whitchurch, shortly before its collapse.

brought the bones of his illustrious ancestor back to Whitchurch, and a magnificent Tomb was erected on the right side of the Chancel. As was later to transpire, it was fortunate that a certain Mr. Dingley gave a full and exact description of this Tomb in his book called *History from Marble*. It was published during the reign of Charles II and includes a detailed sketch of the Tomb. It shows Shrewsbury's recumbent figure in armour, and wearing the Mantle of the Garter. His feet rest upon a couchant talbot, or hound, and these also flank the structure over which stands a massive canopy. Dingley's details are endorsed by Ashmole's notes on Whitchurch Church, now held in the Ashmolean Museum.

Dingley mentions that Talbot's bones lie under the Church Porch and not under the Tomb, but in this respect he was later proved to be wrong. On a still summer's day, the last day of July, 1711, the whole fabric of the Parish Church at Whitchurch collapsed and fell to the ground. Workmen had just been engaged in repairing a crack which had appeared in one of the arches. There was no other symptom of weakness nor warning of danger. So complete was the destruction that

Sketch of Talbot's Tomb at Whitchurch, after restoration by
Adelaide Countess Brownlow in 1874

few of the monumental and other records could be rescued,
but among them was the recumbent figure of Talbot. This
had presumably been protected by the Canopy of the Tomb.

The parishioners immediately set about rebuilding their
church and, by 1723, the work had been completed. Talbot's
effigy had not been disturbed nor was the Canopy replaced.
But the Rector, the Rev. T. Corser, refers to an interesting
discovery in his contemporary notes: [2]

"Whether the bones of the great Talbot were removed from
France or not, it is certain that his heart was brought here for
internment. In rebuilding the church in 1712 the urn was
found which contained his heart embalmed, in a crimson
velvet covering; and the Rector (Mr. Corser) has in his
possession two curious relics of horn, edged with silver . . .
which were taken out of the urn at that time. They belonged

to the beads of the great Lord Talbot and were enclosed in a crimson velvet purse in the urn. They were taken out by a Mr. Maisterson, who was Churchwarden at that period, by whom the urn, with the rest of its contents, was restored to its original resting place" (under the floor of the porch).

These medallions have been handed down and, in 1885, were in the possession of Mr. W. H. Egerton, the then Rector of Whitchurch. What is curious is that they have since been examined several times by antiquarians, all of whom have no hesitation in saying that they could not possibly be earlier than the late sixteenth century. It is therefore a mystery as to how they were added to the contents of the urn.

In the same century Whitchurch passed into the hands of the Brownlows. In 1868 the then Lord Brownlow married Lady Adelaide Talbot, daughter of the 18th Earl of Shrewsbury. By that time the church was again in bad repair and, at Mr. Egerton's suggestion, the Brownlows decided to rectify this and, at the same time, to reconstruct Talbot's tomb in accordance with Mr. Dingley's sketch and description. Late in 1873 the necessary faculty was obtained and Mr. Egerton wrote:

"Upon the removal of the recumbent figure from the cill of the window in order to construct the basement and front of the tomb, the bones were revealed immediately beneath the slab on which the effigy lay. They were not enclosed in a coffin but in what had once been a strong box, three feet by nine and a half inches, which soon crumbled into dust on exposure to the air. It was found that every bone, from the scull to the small metacarpal (bones of the hands) had been carefully wrapped in cere cloth. They were reverently taken by the hand which writes these notes and laid in anatomical order on the Vestry Table. The interest which was taken in the discovery of the bones, not only by the Parishioners, but by all classes in the neighbourhood and by Members of the Society of Antiquaries in London, was very great . . . There lay the mortal frame of the 'English Achilles' who, more than four centuries ago, had fought his country's battles".

And there lay the skull, bearing undoubted evidence of the blow which caused his death. The following is an anatomical description of the bones, attested by Dr. Gwynne, M.D., and Mr. John Bromfield, Surgeon:

Sketch of Talbot's Skull by T. Raffles Davison (from a photograph by J. R. Crosse)

"The neck of the femur was very nearly horizontal. The sagittal suture was completely ossified and not visible. All the others were more or less ossified. Immediately behind the right parietal eminence of the cranium was a perpendicular fracture, evidently caused by a sharp instrument. It was 2¾ inches long and, in the centre ⅝ inches across. About ¾ of an inch of the upper and lower length of the fracture the bone was merely split as by a sharp cut. There was no loss of substance as in the centre.

"One molar tooth in the lower jaw was perfect but almost worn down by use as were three incisors. There were apparently no teeth in the upper jaw . . . the bones generally were remarkably well developed and evidently belonged to a muscular man".

Mr. Egerton remarks that a mouse had made a nest inside the skull and thereby proved a benefactor to history. Had not the cere cloth been gnawed through at the appropriate place, the fatal gash, confirming the exact cause of Talbot's death, would not have been discovered.

On 9th January, 1918, Mr. Fletcher, then Vicar of Shelton and Oxon, Shrewsbury, wrote to General Sir Reginald Talbot in connection with Talbot's Tomb. He added the following post-script:

"A prominent Dentist in Shrewsbury keeps in his Surgery (in a drawer) a double tooth of the Great Earl: it was taken out of the body by a Whitchurch Doctor, who was present when the Tomb was opened, and given to the Dentist. He has shown it to me twice, but I felt sorry that the skeleton was robbed even of a tooth".

On Friday, April 10th, 1874, with a simple ceremony, the bones were deposited within the restored Tomb at the east end of the south aisle of Whitchurch Church.

The Urn containing Talbot's heart lies on, undisturbed, in the Porch.

APPENDIX A

NOTES ABOUT PEOPLE AND PLACES

1. Margaret, Lady Shrewsbury

After the departure of her husband for Bordeaux she still stoutly carried on the struggle against James, 11th Lord Berkeley, for the Berkeley inheritance.

While she was residing at the Manor House of Wooton-under-Edge, Lord Berkeley attacked and looted Painswick Manor. Thereupon Lord Lisle, as has already been related, attacked Berkeley Castle by night, captured Lord Berkeley and his four sons and left them prisoners in his mother's hands, when he sailed to join his father in 1453. Lady Berkeley was already a prisoner of the Talbots, and died that same year. Lord Berkeley subsequently won his release and in 1457 married Joan, Maud Talbot's youngest daughter, who apparently had no love for her Stepmother. However, in 1463 Lord Berkeley executed a Deed of Reconciliation with Margaret. He died a few days later.

On July 23rd, 1454, complaint was made to the King by Sir Bertelot de Riviere and Sir Loys de Bretail, then living in poverty in England, regarding the Shrewsburys' possession of the prisoner Sir Olivier de Cotiny, lately Seneschal of Gascony, who had been taken prisoner by them at the capture of Bordeaux. [1] They claimed that he had been illicitly sent to England by the late Earl of Shrewsbury. Both Plaintiffs had been taken prisoner by the French at Castillon, and they now claimed their right to the possession of Sir Olivier. Margaret appears to have countered by demanding his ransom of 6,000 gold nobles and 100 marks before she would release him. It would seem that this was not forthcoming as, in 1457 John, 2nd Earl of Shrewsbury, who under his father's Will was now in possession of Goodrich Castle and, presumably, of the prisoners in its dungeons, accepted a payment on account for Sir Olivier of 600 gold nobles. [2] This did at last secure his release for, in 1458, he married an illegitimate daughter of King Charles whose dowry was 12,000 gold crowns. [3]

Margaret died in 1467, without gaining the Warwick title and inheritance for which she had fought so hard; it went to her half sister's husband. She was buried in Jesus Chapel of old St. Paul's Cathedral.

2. Thomas Talbot (son of Lord Lisle)

He escaped from Bordeaux and rejoined his mother at Painswick. He

179

England, c. 1450, showing the estates of the chief noble house

was attractive and impulsive. Now Lord Lisle, he re-opened the quarrel with James, Lord Berkeley, his brother-in-law. On March 19th, 1469 he sent Berkeley a taunting challenge to come out of his Castle and settle the inheritance one way or the other by combat. The 1463 Deed of Reconciliation seems to have been ignored.

Berkeley answered promptly by return of Herald telling Thomas to meet him next day at Nibley Green where "the trouth shall be showed by the marcy of God" (sic). Of the details of this battle, the last ever fought in England between private armies, little is known.

But that it was a fierce little affair is clear from the discovery near Nibley Church of a communal grave containing 150 skeletons.

For an instant in the battle Thomas raised the visor of his helmet. In that moment he fell from his horse, an arrow quivering in his cheek. He was stabbed to death by a Berkeley retainer. The shock of his death was too great for his young wife. Sixteen days later she had a miscarriage.

So ended the male line of Shrewsbury's family by his second wife.

3. Shrewsbury's children

Maud's sons:

Thomas —died before his father (probably as an infant).

John — succeeded as 2nd Earl, slain at Northampton 1460, direct ancestor of the present Earl.

Christopher — also slain at Northampton 1460.

Margaret's sons and daughters:

John, Lord Lisle of Kingston Lisle in Berkshire—killed at Castillon. Thomas succeeded him but was killed 1469 (see above).

Humphrey — Marshal of Calais, died 1492, at Mount Sinai.

Lewis was seated at Perryard in Herefordshire.

Joan became the fourth wife of James, Lord Berkeley, who died in 1463 and she then married again.

Eleanor was alleged by Richard III to have married Edward IV in secret. She became the wife of Sir Thomas Butler, Lord Sudeley (vide Will, Appendix B)

Henry — there is no record of the name of the mother of this illegitimate son. He too was killed at Castillon.

There is no mention of "Wariss" other than in Shrewsbury's Will.

4. Goodrich Castle

Goodrich Castle still stands as a majestic ruin on the brow of the hill overlooking the River Wye. The nucleus is pre-Norman and the general plan is that of a parallelogram flanked by massive, red sandstone towers at the angles. It is surrounded on the landward side by a deep moat hewn out of the solid rock. Adjoining the narrow entrance passage and parallel to it was the Chapel, part of which John Talbot reconstructed.

The North Tower, called the Ladies Tower, contained the State Rooms and these too were reconstructed by him. The Great State Room was 55 feet by 20 feet and at the top were two beautifully pointed arches springing from an octagonal pillar in the centre.

The Great Hall was 60 feet by 30 feet and a deep well stood in the centre making the Castle virtually independent of outside water supply, and thus impregnable to siege.

The Norman Keep had three floors, and a dungeon underground for prisoners.

When resident in the Castle, John Talbot slept on the first floor of the Keep which was regarded as his special room.

The Castle came into Talbot hands in 1328, together with Painswick and other Manors, through Elizabeth Comyn, the wife of Richard, 2nd Baron Talbot. Elizabeth was an heiress of that Countess of Pembroke who founded Pembroke College, Oxford. On the death of her grandfather in 1324, the Dispensers, long enemies of the Comyns, abducted Elizabeth and held her prisoner in their castle at Purfrith while they brought every pressure to bear on her to make Goodrich over to them. In the end she gave in but that did not win the poor girl's release.

In 1328 Sir Richard Talbot heard of her plight. He dramatically rescued Elizabeth and took her back to Goodrich where they were married. Richard was John's great grandfather.

In 1646 during the Civil War, Colonel Birch, the Parliamentary leader, invested the Castle but never captured it. With the cessation of warfare on the Welsh Marches, Goodrich's strength became unnecessary and its decay was hastened when the well went dry. By the time of Henry VIII it appears to have ceased to have any great significance.

6. Blackmere or Blakemere Castle

All that now remains is a grassy mound on the south side of the Mere, one of several in the area around Whitchurch. The house was a Manor rather than a Castle but was, nevertheless, substantial.

Accounts for the years 1394 to 1425 have been preserved and form part of the Bridgewater Collection in Salop Record Office.

The Castle was first occupied by the Le Strange family in the early part of the twelfth century. Ankaret, John Talbot's mother, who brought the Lordship of Blackmere (i.e., Whitchurch) with her, was evidently much attached to it, and it would seem from the accounts that she and the children spent as much time as possible there.

The Castle was sold in 1590 but by 1695 it is described as being "almost quite a ruin".

APPENDIX B

JOHN TALBOT'S WILL

The reference at Somerset House is 311 b Kempe, and is dated at Portsmouth, Friday 1st September, 1452:

"In the name of our Lord God, Amen. I, John Earl of Shrewsbury, Wexford and Waterford, Lord Talbot, Furnival and Strange, whole of body and in my good mind, being this Friday, the first day of September the year of our Lord 1452 at Portsmouth make and dispose my Testament and Last Will in this manner.

"First I bequeath my Soul to Almighty God my Creator and to our Lady Saint Mary and to all the Saints in Heaven and my body to be buried at Blackmere in the Parish Church on the right side of the Chancel where I wish to be built a chapel of Our Lady and Saint George for me at my cost and charge. Also I will and ordain that there be a College founded* in the said Church to the value of £40 per year over the value of the parsonage of the said Church and that the said parsonage and other Churches go to the foundation of the said College to pray for me and my wife and all our Children, Ancestors and all our good doers;

or else to be buried in the College of Warwick in the New Chapel there which Richard, late Earl of Warwick, my Father in Law late doth make and ordain in case that any time hereafter I may attain to the name, and Lordship of Warwick as of right.

"Also I will and grant and freely ordain that my wife have and enjoy the Lordships of Blackmere, Whitchurch, Dudington and Lynvall in the County of Salop, the Manor and Lordship of Merbury in Cheshire and the Manor and Lordship of Painswick with the appurtenance in the Shire of Gloucester after the form and tenure of a fine . . . thereupon in the Kings Court, that is to say to me and to her and to the heirs of our two bodies, lawfully begotten, as in the fine more plainly it appeareth.

"Also I will and grant and fully ordain that my son the Viscount Lisle shall have the Castle and Lordship of Pynyarde and the Manor of Credenhill with the appurtenance in the Shire of Hereford and the Manor of Strangeford with the Lordship of Irchenfield with the appurtenance, to him and to his heirs of his body lawfully begotten.

"And if he die without issue of his body lawfully begotten, I will

---

*This was never done, probably because no money was forthcoming from the crown. (Editor).

that the said Castle and Manors fully remain unto my son Sir Lewis and to the heirs of his body lawfully begotten.

"And if the said Lewis die without issue of his body lawfully begotten I will that the said Castle and Manors wholly remain unto my son Humphrey his brother and to the heirs of his body lawfully begotten.

"And if the said Humphrey die without issue of his body lawfully begotten I will that the said Castle and Manors wholly remain unto the right heirs of me for evermore as in a Deed thereof made more plainly it appeareth.

"Also I will and ordain that my son the Viscount Lisle have the Castle and Manor of the Cheswarden, the Manor of Wroxwarden and Sutton Madok in the Shire of Salop with their appurtenances to him and to his heirs of his body lawfully begotten, and the manor of Tassely in the said Shire to him and to his heirs for evermore, as in their Deeds and Evidence thereof made more plainly it appeareth.

"Moreover I will and grant and fully ordain that my wife have wholly her Dower of all my income due to me as a soldier without any interruption.

"Also I will and grant and fully ordain and devise that my wife have after my decease two places of my purchased lands in Shrewsbury and also two places of my purchased lands in Ludlow for tenure of her life and after her decease will that my son the Viscount Lisle have one of the places in Shrewsbury which he will chose and to his heirs and my son Sir Lewis the other to him and to his heirs.

"And as to my places in Ludlow my son Sir Lewis to have them to him and to his heirs for evermore.

"Also I will that my son Sir Lewis have the Castle of Corsham and Culmington for term of his life. And also that my said son Sir Lewis and my son Humphrey his brother have and enjoy all my purchased lands in Shropshire and other places after the form and effect of divers Deeds and evidences thereof made, unto them as in the said Deeds and Evidences more plainly appeareth.

"And also my said son Sir Lewis shall have my purchased lands and houses in Hampshire to him and to his heirs for evermore.

"Also I will that my son and heir* have the Lordships of Goodrich and Irchenfield and all the remnant of Talbots and Stranges income except the gifts and grants before reserved. And also all my income in Ireland and France and Normandy as it appeareth by the King's Patents made thereof except those that were given to me and to my wife and to my children as it appeareth by the King's Patents thereof made.

"Also I will and grant and fully ordain that my son, Sir Lewis, have

---

*This is the only reference to his eldest son by Maud.

all my terms which I have in the form of the Manor and Lordship of Glossop by the grant of the Abbot of Basinwerk.

"Also I will that Thomas Everyngham have his 'fee' of £10 to hold for term of his life of my grant. And that John Evans have his 'fee' at Middleton for term of his life. And that John Gye have his office of Constable of Goodrich Castle for term of his life with the fee belonging thereto.

"Also I will grant and fully ordain that my wife have her clothing that belongeth to her body and to her head, with all such things as I have given her before this time without any claim or interruption of my Executors or of my children, and also all such vessels of silver as bear my Arms and hers together or the Dog or the Ragged Staff.

"Also I will that my wife have all the remnants of my movable goods paying for my other goods as may be agreed between her and my Executors.

"And the money thereof to be paid for acquitting of my debts and rewarding of my servants after the discretion of my executors.

"Also I will that my wife have a Ship called the *Margaret* and a barge called the *Christopher* of which John Prat is Master, and also the share I have in the *Nicholas* of the . . . And I will that my wife have the vessels aforesaid with the apparel that goes with them.

"And as to the £1000 that is paid for my daughter Eleanor's marriage in case the Covenants be not performed on the Lord Sudeley's part that then my Executors sue for the repayment of the aforesaid sum against the said Lord Sudeley.

"Also I will and ordain that the Lordships of Rampton, Swindon, Shrivenham, Broughton and Ashton stand still in their hands that are enfieffed therein. And the issues and profits of all the said Lordships go to the payment of my debts and performance of my Will until my debts be fully paid as well for the marriage of my Daughter, Wariss, as for the remnant of my Will performed.

"Also I will that my wife, and my Executors sue the King and Lords of his Council for such debts as are due to me by our said Sovereign Lord considering the great cost and injury to my person that I have had in his service that my wife and my executors may have my said debts in performing my Will without which it cannot be done.

"Also I will that my son, Sir Lewis have a ship called the *Carwell* with all the apparel and my son Humphrey to have a ship called the *Gregeo* with all the apparel which goes with it.

"And this my will to be done and performed I make and ordain my wife, William Gatesby, John Brown, N. Byllying, William Northingham, William Cumberforde, Thomas Everingham, and Roger Stedman, my Executors whom I require and charge as they will answer before God to execute this my Will. And especially I pray and require my son and heir and on my blessing as highly as I can, as the Father may charge the Son in "(aiming?)" of my "(curse?)", and as he will have my blessing I charge him that he intercept not nor hinder the performance of this my Will, and neither he nor any other of my blood and if they or any of them do hinder this Will that then my fiefs make a statement of such lands as they have been enfieffed in to my Executors and they to sell the said lands and dispose them for me.

"And to oversee the execution of this my Testament and last Will I have ordained and by this my Will I require and beseech to be overseer the Bishop of Winchester, the Bishop of Hereford, and the Earl of Worcester and my son the Viscount Lisle to take upon them the oversight and fulfilling thereof.

"Written the day and year aforesaid and signed by my own hand and closed and sealed with my Seal at Portsmouth abovesaid".

Shewsbury

Note

The Bishop of Winchester was William of Waynfleet, first Provost of Eton and founder of Magdalen College, Oxford.

The Bishop of Hereford was Reginald Boulers.

The Earl of Worcester was Sir John Tiptoft, whose father had fought alongside John in France 1429-36.

APPENDIX C

VIDE CHAPTER XI

Certificate of payments made to Henry Armoure and Richard Vernon at Mantes, 28th August, 1441.

In the year 1441, the 28th day of August, before us, Thomas Hoo, Knight, bailly of Mantes, appeared personally Henry Armoure and Richard Vernon, men-at-arms, who owned and acknowledged that they had had and received of Pierre Baille, Receiver-General of Normandy, the sum of 14 livres, ten sols, Tournois, which Monseigneur de Talbot, Marshal of France, had in our presence commanded to be paid to them by the said Receiver for the causes hereafter declared. That is to say:

To the said Henry, 10 livres, Tournois, for his trouble and pay in having at this time gone hastily from the town of Mantes to the Town of Pontoise, to ascertain the position of the Lords and the other subjects of the King, our Lord, who are there, and from the said place of Pontoise to Conflans to enquire, see and ascertain the condition and the army of the chief adversary of the King, our said Lord, who is at the said place of Conflans, and to report upon the whole to my said Lord de Talbot, in order that he may the better dispose of the army under him in this said town for the victualling of the said place of Pontoise and perform many other exploits of war, and to the said Richard, four livres, ten sols Tournois, for his trouble and wages in going from this said town to the said place of Pontoise to enquire about the condition of the Lords and other subjects of the King, our said Lord, who are there, and to convey a speedy answer to my said Lord de Talbot. Of the which sum the said Henry and Richard consider themselves satisfied and well paid, and thereof they would acquit, and do acquit by these presents, the King, our said Lord, the said Receiver General and all others.

Dated at Mantes under our signet in the year and day above written.

And for the greater confidence and security hereof we have hereto caused to be affixed the seal of the town and jurisdiction of the Castle of Mantes, by the Keeper of the same, on the year and day above said.

LE COMTE

APPENDIX D

Money Values and Wages

1. TABLE OF COINS AND MONEY VALUES

(Wylie, *The History of England under Henry IV*, Vol. IV, App. T)

ENGLISH COINS

Silver:

1 Penny or Sterling (with Half Pence and Farthings)

1 Groat (4 Pennies) (with Half Groats)

Gold:

1 Ferling or Quarter Noble = 20 Pence (written 1s.8d.)

1 Mail or Half Noble = 40 Pence (written 3s.4d.)

A "Mark", which was not a coin, was 160 Pence written 13s.4d.

FRENCH COINS

1 French Penny	= 1 English Half Penny
1 Blanc	= 2/3rds English Penny
1 Franc or Crown	= 3s. 4d.
1 Gold Franc	= 16s.

All large sums of money were written in £. s. d. or Marks. Coinage suffered continuous debasement (notably in 1412). In 1265 the weight of the penny had been fixed at 32 grains of dry wheat. By 1412 this had been reduced to 15. Similarly, the amount of gold in a Noble was reduced from 45 Nobles per lb. in 1351 to 50 in 1412.

2. APPROXIMATE WAGE LEVELS, 1420

(a) Service in War (Newhall, *English Conquest of Normandy*, p.156):

Dukes	13/6d. per day
Earls	6/8d. per day
Barons	4/-d. per day
Knights	2/-d. per day
Men-at-arms	1/-d. per day
Archers	6d. per day

(b) Civilians (Jacob, p.385)

Carvers and Joiners	7½d. per day	They worked 5 1/3rd days per week
Carpenters	5½d. per day	
Masons	5½d. per day	
Mason's Mates	4¼d. per day	
Agricultural Worker	3½d. per day	

3. INCOME STRATA

E. F. Jacob, *The Fifteenth Century,* p.333, gives the following rough
evaluation of various income levels based on taxation data for 1436.

Duke of York	£3,231 per annum
Earl of Warwick	£3,116 per annum
Duke of Gloucester	£2,243 per annum
Earl of Suffolk	£1,667 per annum
Earl of Stafford	£855 per annum

51 Barons average £768 to £865 per annum
183 Greater Knights average £208 per annum
750 Lesser Knights average £40 – £100 per annum
1,200 Taxpayers average £20 – £35 per annum
1,600 Taxpayers average £10 – £19 per annum

Taxation was graded from 6d. in the Pound on incomes between £5
and £100; up to 2/-d. in the Pound on the higher income brackets.

BIBLIOGRAPHY

Baddeley, W. St. Clair, *A Cotswold Manor (Painswick)*, London, 1907

Bland, D. S., *Early Records of Furnival's Inn*, Newcastle, 1957

Bullough, Geoffrey, *Narrative and Dramatic Sources of Shakespeare*, Routledge & Kegan Paul, London, 1957-75

Burne, Lieut. Col. A.H., *The Agincourt War*, London, 1956

Chartier, Jean, *Chronique de Charles VII*, ed. Vallet de Viriville, Paris, 1858

Chartier, Jean, Berry, Matthieu de Coucy et Autres Historiens, *Histoire de Charles VII*, Paris, 1661

Cousinot, Guillaume, *Les Gestes de Nobles Français*, ed. Vallet de Viriville in *La Chronique de la Pucelle*. Paris 1859

Curtis, E., *Medieval Ireland from 1086 to 1513*, London, 1938

D'Alton, John, *Memoirs of the Archbishops of Dublin*, Dublin, 1838

d'Escouchy, Matthieu, *Chronicles*, ed. G. du Fresne de Beaucourt, Paris, 1863

Egerton, the Rev. W. J. "*Talbot's Tomb*". Published in *Transactions of the Shropshire Archeological and Natural History Society*, 1885 and 1887.

Froissart, Sir John. *Chronicles*. Translated from the original French at the command of King Henry VIII by John Bourchier, Lord Berners, reprinted from Pynson's Edition of 1523 and 1525, London, 1812

Fuller, Thomas, *The Church-History of Britain*, London, 1655

Gilbert, J. T., *History of Viceroys of Ireland*, Dublin, 1865

Green, V.H.H., *The Later Plantagenets*, Edward Arnold, London, 1955 (1962 edition)

Gruel, Guillaume, *Chronique d'Arthur de Richemont*, ed. A.L. Vavasseur, *Soc. Hist. France*, Paris, 1890

Hall, Edward, *The Union of two noble and Illustre families of Lancaster and Yorke*, 1548. ed. Henry Ellis, London, 1809

Hardyng, John, *Chronicles*, London, 1653

Holinshed, *Chronicles*, Second Edition 1587, London, 1808

Hunter, Joseph, *Hallamshire*, London, 1819

Jacob, E.F., *The Fifteenth Century, 1399-1485*, Oxford, 1961 (1969 edition)

MacFarlane, K.B., *John Wycliffe and the beginning of English Nonconformity*, London, 1952 (eighth edition)

Monstrelet, Enguerrand de, *Chronicles*, translated by Thomas Johnes, printed at the Hasod Press, 1809

Nashe, Thomas, *Complete Works*, 1592 ("Pierce Penilesse his suppli-cation to the Divell," ed. by R.B. McKerrow, 1798, Oxford (1966 edition)

Newhall, R.A., *English Conquest of Normandy, 1416-24*, London, 1924

Ralegh Radford, C.A., *Goodrich Castle*, Ministry of Works Official Guide Book, H M Stationery Office, 1958

Robinson, Rev. C.J., *A History of the Castles of Herefordshire and their Lords*, London, 1869

Rymer's *Foedera*, Vols VII to XII, 2nd. edition, Churchill, London, 1704-1732

Sackville-West, Miss V., *Saint Joan of Arc*, London, 1936

Shakespeare, William. *Henry IV, Part 1*. New Penguin Edition, ed. P.H. Davison (1978 edition)

Steel, A.B., *The Receipt of the Exchequer, 1377-1485*, Cambridge, 1954

Stevenson, J., *Letters and Papers Illustrative of the Wars of the English in France. Henry VI. Rolls Series*, London, 1861-1864

Strickland, Miss E., *Lives of the Queens of England*, Vol III, London, 1841

Thevet, G. A., *Vrais portraits des hommes Illustres* (Book IV), Paris, 1584

Usk, Adam, *Chronicon*, 1352-1430, ed. E.M. Thompson, London, 1876

Vickers, K.H., *Humphrey Duke of Gloucester*, London, 1907

Walsingham, Thomas of, *Historia Anglicana* (Vol II), ed. H.T. Riley, London, 1864

Waugh, W.T., *Sir John Oldcastle, E.H.R.*, Vol. XX, London, 1905

Waurin, Jean du Forestal, *Receveil de Chroniques et Anchiennes Istories de la Grant Bretagne á present nommé Engleterre* (Vols 3-7) Rolls Series, ed. and translated W. and E.L.C.P. Hardy, London, 1884-1891

White, Robert, *The Dukeries Records*, Printed privately for sub-scribers. Worksop, 1904 (Bodleian)

Williams, Miss E. Carlton, *My Lord of Bedford*, London, 1963

Worcester, William of (1415-82), *Annales Rerum Anglicarum*, ed. T. Hearne, Oxford, 1728

Wylie, J.H., *The History of England under Henry IV* (4 Vols), London, 1884-98
The Reign of Henry V (3 Vols), Cambridge, 1914-29

SOURCE NOTES

Chapter I

1 Ralegh Radford, *Goodrich Castle*, p.3.
2. *Vrais Portraits des Hommes Illustres*, Book IV, p.282.
3. "Talbot's Tomb", *Transactions of the Shropshire Archaeological and Natural History Society*, Vol. III (111), p.413 et seq.
4. Hardyng, *Chronicles*, Ch. LXCIII.
5. Froissart, *Chronicles*, Vol. II, Ch. CCXIX.
6. *Ibid.*, Ch. CCXXIV.
7. *Ibid.*, Ch. CCXIV.
8. Hunter, *Hallamshire*, p.44.
9. *History of Viceroys of Ireland*, p.278.
10. *Ibid.*, p.280.
11. *Ibid.*, p.283.
12. *Ibid.*, p.284.
13. *Ibid.*, p.287.
14. *Ibid.*, p.285.
15. Wylie, *The History of England under Henry IV*, Vol.I, p.92.
16. Holinshed, *Chronicles*, Vol.III, p.2.

Chapter II

1. Gilbert, *op. cit.*, p.287.
2. Holinshed, *op. cit.*, p.17.
3. Wylie, *op. cit.*, p.199.
4. Curtis, *Medieval Ireland*, p.286.
5. Newhall, *English Conquest of Normandy*, p.156.
6. Rymer's *Foedera*, Vol. VIII, p.279.
7. *Ibid.*, p.291.
8. Strickland, *Lives of the Queens of England*, Vol. III, p.120.
9. Hall, *The Union of two noble and Illustre families of Lancaster and Yorke*, p.30.
10. Wylie, *op. cit.*, Vol. IV, Appendix G.

Chapter III

1. Green, *The Later Plantagenets*, p.253.
2. Wylie, *op cit.*, Vol. III, p.112.
3. *Ibid.*, p.152.

4. *Ibid.*, p.266.
5. *Ibid.*, p.288.
6. Holinshed, *op. cit.*, p.65.
7. Wylie, *op. cit.*, Vol. III, p.319.
8. Rymer's *Foedora*, Vol. IX, p.61.
9. *Ibid.*, p.120.
10. *Ibid.*, p.119.
11. Gilbert, *op. cit.*, p.304.
12. Williams, *My Lord of Bedford*, p.138.
13. Wylie, *op. cit.*, Vol. I, p.64.
14. Rymer's *Foedora*, Vol. IX, p.238.

Chapter IV

1. Curtis, *op cit.*, p.291.
2. Gilbert, *op cit.*, p.304.
3. *Ibid.*, p.306.
4. *Ibid.*, p.304.
5. Curtis, *op cit.*, p.231.
6. Gilbert, *op cit.*, p.300.
7. Curtis, *op cit.*, p.288.
8. Gilbert, *op cit.*, p.304.
9. Curtis, *op cit.*, p.385.
10. Gilbert, *op cit.*, p.304.
11. *Ibid.*, p.305.
12. *Ibid.*, p.305.
13. Curtis, *op cit.*, p.294.
14. *Ibid.*, p.295.
15. Waurin, *Receveil*, Vol. V, p.201.
16. Curtis, *op cit.*, p.291.
17. Wylie, *The Reign of Henry V*, Vol. I, p.67.
18. Holinshed, *op cit.*, p.85.
19. D'Alton, *Memoirs of the Archbishops of Dublin*, p.152.
20. Gilbert, *op cit.*, p.306.
21. *Ibid.*, p.307.
22. British Museum. Coth MS Titus BXI, Part I, ff.31.46.
23. D'Alton, *op cit.*, p.154.
24. Gilbert, *op cit.*, p.310.

Chapter V

1. Gilbert, *op cit.*, p.311.
2. Monstrelet, *Chronicles*, Vol. II, Ch. CXI.
3. White, *The Dukeries Records*, p.303.
4. Hall, *op cit.*, p.105.

5. Cal. Close Rolls. Henry V 1421.
6. Gilbert, *op cit.*, p.315.
7. *Ibid.*, p.316.
8. *Ibid.*, p.317.
9. Hall, *op cit.*, p.111.

Chapter VI

1. Hall, *op cit.*, p.112.
2. Rymer's *Foedora*, Vol. X, p.253.
3. *Ibid.*, p.254.
4. Jacob, *The Fifteenth Century*, p.212.
5. Cal. Close Rolls. Henry VI 1423.
6. Newhall, *op cit.*, p.305.
7. Williams, *op cit.*, p.110.
8. Berkeley MSS (Bristol and Gloucester Archaeological Society), Vol. II, pp.29 and 95.
9. Waurin, *op cit.*, Vol. V, p.44.
10. Newhall, *op cit.*, p.319.
11. Williams, *op cit.*, p.116.
12. Gilbert, *op cit.*, p.321.
13. Jacob, *op cit.*, p.229.
14. Monstrelet, *op cit.*, Vol. II, Ch. CLXXXVII.
15. Rymer's *Foedora*, Vol. X, p.387.
16. Vickers, *Humphrey Duke of Gloucester*, p.176.
17. Williams, *op cit.*, p.140.
18. *Ibid.*, p.141.
19. *Ibid.*, p.142.
20. Hall, *op cit.*, p.137.
21. Williams, *op cit.*, p.146.
22. *Ibid.*, p.149.

Chapter VII

1. Williams, *op cit.*, p.149.
2. Holinshed, *op cit.*, p.156.
3. Hall, *op cit.*, p.129.
4. Waurin, *op cit.*, Vol. III, p.221.
5. Hall, *op cit.*, p.143.
6. Waurin, *op cit.*, Vol. V, p.154.
7. Williams, *op cit.*, p.157.
8. Waurin, *op cit.*, Vol. V, p.154.
9. Williams, *op cit.*, p.158.
10. Monstrelet, *op cit.*, Vol. III, Ch. CCIII.
11. Burne, *The Agincourt War*, p.229.

12. Williams, *op cit.*, p.161.
13. Chartier, *Chronique de Charles VII*, Vol. I, p.18.
14. Chartier et al., *Histoire de Charles VII*, p.508.
15. Holinshed, *op cit.*, p.162.
16. Williams, *op cit.*, p.165.

Chapter VIII

1. Monstrelet, *op cit.*, Vol. II, Ch. CCX.
2. Sackville-West, *Saint Joan of Arc*, p.199.
3. *Ibid.*, p.211.
4. Chartier, *op cit.*, Vol. I, p.79.
5. Sackville-West, *op cit.*, p.219.
6. Burne, *op cit.*, p.251.
7. Sackville-West, *op cit.*, p.221.
8. Waurin, *op cit.*, Vol. V, p.177.
9. *Ibid.*, p.180.
10. *Ibid.*, p.181.
11. Sackville-West, *op cit.*, p.223.
12. Waurin, *op cit*, Vol. V, p.185.

Chapter IX

1. Waurin, *op cit.*, Vol. V, p.189.
2. Hall, *op cit.*, p.150.
3. William of Worcester, *Annales*, Vol. I, p.422.
4. Sackville-West, *op cit.*, p.286.
5. Holinshed, *op cit.*, p.174.
6. Rymer's Foedora, Vol X, p.537
7. Holinshed, *op cit.*, p.176.
8. Hall, *op cit.*, p.170.
9. Stevenson, *Letters and Papers*, Vol. II, Part II, p.540.
10. Holinshed, *op cit.*, p.182.
11. Monstrelet, *op cit.*, Vol. III, Ch. LXXX.
12. *Ibid.*, Ch. LXXXV.
13. *Ibid.*, Ch. LXXXI.
14. *Ibid.*, Ch. CXL.

Chapter X

1. Holinshed, *op cit.*, p.185.
2. Monstrelet, *op cit.*, Vol. III, Ch. XCVIII.
3. Waurin, *op cit.*, Vol. V, p.217.
4. William of Worcester, *Annales*, Vol. II, p.286.
5. Monstrelet, *op cit.*, Vol. III, Ch. CXIII.

6. Hall, *op cit.*, p.180.
7. Monstrelet, *op cit.*, Vol. III, Ch. CXXIV.
8. Holinshed, *op cit.*, p.193.
9. Chartier, *op cit.*, p.93.
10. Hall, *op cit.*, p.188.
11. Waurin, *op cit.*, Vol. V, p.239.
12. Burne, *op cit.*, p.286.
13. Holinshed, *op cit.*, p.194.
14. Monstrelet, *op cit.*, Vol. III, Ch. CXLI.
15. Hall, *op cit.*, p.189.
16. Waurin, *op cit.*, Vol. V, p.259.

Chapter XI

1. *Painswick* (official guide), p.25.
2. William of Worcester, *Annales,* Vol. II, p.317.
3. Holinshed, *op cit.*, p.199.
4. *Ibid.*, p.203.
5. Hall, *op cit.*, p.193.
6. Holinshed, *op cit.*, p.196.
7. Monstrelet, *op cit.*, Vol. III, Ch. CLXI.
8. Waurin, *op cit.*, Vol V, p.320.
9. William of Worcester, *op cit.*, p.605.
10. Monstrelet, *op cit.*, Vol. III, Ch. CLXI.
11. Waurin, *op cit.*, p.323.
12. Hall, *op cit.*, p.191.
13. *Ibid.*, p.191.
14. *Ibid.*, p.192.
15. Chartier, *op cit.*, p.117.
16. *Transactions of the Shropshire Archaeological and Natural History Society,* Part II, Vol. VIII, p.427.

Chapter XII

1. Strickland, *Lives of the Queens of England,* Vol. III, p.223.
2. Baddeley, *op cit.*, p.105.
3. Bland, *Early Records of Furnival's Inn.*
4. *Gilbert, op cit.*, p.388.
5. William of Worcester,*Annales,* Vol. I, p.431.
6. Holinshed, *op cit.*, p.197.
7. Hall, *op cit.*, p.195.
8. Strickland, *op cit.*, p.223.
9. Stevenson, *op cit.*, Vol. II, p.598.
10. *Ibid.*, Vol. I, p.87 et seq.
11. *Ibid.*, p.103.

12. *Ibid.*, p.116.
13. Gilbert, *op cit.*, p.348.
14. D'Alton, *op cit.*, p.158.
15. Curtis, *op cit.*, p.303.
16. *Ibid.*, p.307.
17. Gilbert, *op cit.*, p.348.
18. Curtis, *op cit.*, p.307.
19. Waurin, *op cit.*, Vol. VI, p.121.
20. Stevenson, *op cit.*, Vol. I, p.496.
21. *Ibid.*, p.498.
22. William of Worcester, *Annales*, Vol. II, p,718.
23. *Ibid.*, p.735.

Chapter XIII

1. Waurin, *op cit.*, Vol. VI, p.139.
2. *Ibid.*, p.141.
3. *Ibid.*, p.142.
4. *Ibid.*, p.145.
5. Chartier, *Histoire de Charles VII*, p.591.
6. Waurin, *op cit.*, p.163.
7. d'Escouchy, *Chronicles*, Vol. III, p.376.
8. Chartier, *op cit.*, Vol. II, p.226.
9. Wylie, *The Reign of Henry V*, Vol. III, p.72.
10. d'Escouchy, *op cit.*, Vol. I, p.23, n.2.
11. Stevenson, *op cit.*, Vol. II, p.735.
12. Waurin, *op cit.*, Vol. VI, p.160.

Chapter XIV

1. Green, *The Later Plantagenets*, p.280.
2. Waurin, *op cit.*, Vol. VI, p.179.
3. Monstrelet, *op cit.*, Vol. III, Ch. CCXIII.
4. *Ibid.*
5. Rymer's *Foedora*, Vol. XI, p.313.
6. Stevenson, *op cit.*, Vol. II, p.497.
7. *Ibid.*, p.498.
8. Holinshed, *op cit.*, Vol. III, p.228.
9. Rymer's *Foedora*, Vol. XI, p.321.
10. Stevenson, *op cit.*, Vol. II, p.479.
11. Chartier, *Histoire de Charles VII*, Vol. III, p.229.
12. d'Escouchy, *op cit.*, Vol. II, p.35.

Chapter XV

1. Burne, *op cit.*, p.335 et seq.
2. d'Escouchy, *op cit.*, Vol. II, p.41.
3. *Ibid.*, p.39.
4. *Ibid.*, p.41, n.1.
5. *Ibid.*, p.43.

Postscript

1. Chartier, *Histoire de Charles VII*, Vol. III, p.234.
2. *Transactions of the Shropshire Archaeological and Natural History Society*, Part III, Vol. VIII, p.413 et seq. and Vol. X, p.416 et seq.

Appendix A

1. Stevenson, *op cit.*, Vol. II, p.497.
2. Monstrelet, *op cit.*, Vol. III, p.495.
3. d'Escouchy, *op cit.*, Vol. II, p.29, n.4.

INDEX

199